Take my yoke upon you and learn from me.
Matthew 11:29

THE LIBERATING CONNECTION

and

25 Other Discursive Sermon-Essays

Frederick A. Roblee

FAIRWAY PRESS
DRAWER L • LIMA, OHIO 45802

THE LIBERATING CONNECTION AND 25 OTHER DISCURSIVE SERMON-ESSAYS

FIRST EDITION
Copyright © 1984 by
Frederick A. Roblee

All rights reserved. No portion of this book may be reproduced or utilized in any form or by any means, electronic or mechanical including photocopying, without permission in writing from the author.

All Scripture quotations are from the
Revised Standard Version (RSV) unless otherwise indicated.

7521/ISBN 0-89536-978-8   PRINTED IN U.S.A. BY FAIRWAY PRESS

To my wife
Grace Godron Roblee
and to our daughter
Grace Jean Roblee

CONTENTS

Preface vii

Introduction ix

1. The Liberating Connection 1

2. From the Known into the Unknown 10
   (New Year)

3. The Road, Through Doubt, to Faith 17

4. God Has a Plan for Our Lives 24

5. Bible — Word and Spirit 31

6. Why Pray? 39

7. The Human Being 46

8. The Living God 54

9. Jesus Christ — THE INCARNATION 62

10. What Kind of Person Was Jesus? 68
    (With a Reporter in Galilee)

11. Confrontation at the Summit 77
    (Palm Sunday)

12. Body and Blood, Bread and Wine 85
    (Maundy Thursday)

13. He Trusted in God 91
    (Good Friday)

14. Our Risen Lord 96
    (Easter)

15. The Meaning of the Cross for Us 103

16. For Christ's Sake 112

17. Loving and Being Loved 119
    (Mother's Day)

18. Men, Women and God 127

19. The Holy Spirit and the Day of Pentecost 135

20. The Lord's Vineyard 142
    (Independence Day)

21. Can a Rich Man Get into Heaven? 150

22. Our Two Incomes 158

23. Work and Life — Life and Work 166
    (Labor Day)

24. Instead of the Thorn 173

25. America's Thanksgiving Day 181

26. The Kingdom, the Power and the Glory 190

A Discussion Outline Follows Each Sermon-Essay

PREFACE

Preaching has never been more important than it is now in the nineteen eighties. As an institution in American society, the Church depends upon it. And today, the Church, as the *koinonia* (the faith community around Jesus Christ), is more demanding than ever of the one who stands in the pulpit week after week. His or her presence there before the congregation and as the pastor in the homes of the parish, the personal counselor in the study, and a resource person for the congregation and the community make the clergyperson's role as demanding and as difficult as it is also rewarding in divine and human service.

For those with ears to hear and eyes to see, God's *judgment* is written large across every newspaper, magazine and telecast.

> "For my thoughts are not your thoughts,
> neither are your ways my ways
> says the Lord." (Isaiah 55:8)

God's *mercy* is shown in our redemption and forgiveness, and in the renewal of strength, hope and joy. *Faith* and *assurance* are two of the most needed and deeply desired assets to have as we face and live each new day. They make the great difference.

These sermon-essays are accurately described as "discursive," that is, analytical and interpretive. They also cover a wide range of personal and social concerns with *positive Christian faith and hope*, and with an openmindedness toward divergent views. Discussion outlines follow each sermon-essay and will be useful for discussion groups after the service of worship or at any time. These outlines also will help individual readers to come to their own conclusions and commitments.

After many years and with wide experience in the pulpit, in counseling and in ecumenical relationships I realize how much the views of others, whether critical or supportive, have enriched my own life, thoughts and ministry. It is, therefore, with a sense of personal indebtedness that I share with others that which has been most helpful to me in *comprehending* and *living out* the Christian faith and experience.

As I write I think of seminarians and of my fellow ministers and hope that what they find here may be helpful to them in their personal lives, and in sermon preparation. Also I hope that among students and the laity in our churches who read these discussions many will be encouraged in seeing that strong faith is not incompatible with reason, science and intellectual integrity.

Frederick A. Roblee
1984
Springfield, Illinois

INTRODUCTION

In presenting a book of discursive sermon-essays, it is important for the writer to set forth, in broad outline, something of his intellectual perceptions and spiritual experience. The following is my personal affirmation of faith. It is the premise for the discourses which follow.

1. I believe in the eternal God whose essence is spiritual and who, in ways very far beyond our comprehension, created the universe in all its physical and spiritual dimensions, and continues to create and sustain it.*

2. I believe that I, as a human being, am the result of all the complex factors in my inheritance, environment and personal response. I am much more than my biological inheritance. I am also much more than the product of the physical and social environments into which I was born and have lived. In addition to these there has been and remains the fact of my personal response, that is, my feelings, thoughts and decisions. I believe that to a remarkable degree I, like others, am able to take control of my life. I believe that self-control, which is the essence of personal freedom, is a fact of living experience which disproves any theory of complete determinism.

3. I believe that there is a universal framework of existence and that at its center is God's relationship with us and our relationship with him. I also believe that in this spiritual potentiality God has, from time to time, especially revealed himself and that his greatest and normative revelation is the historic life, teaching, death and resurrection of Jesus Christ. I must speak, therefore, of the presence in my life of God-in-Jesus Christ and God-in-the Holy Spirit, not as separate realities or entities but as necessary ways of expressing more completely the whole truth.

4. I believe that Jesus Christ was fully human and at the same time brought, as an historic event, the fullness of God's

---

*For one who wishes to delve into this fundamental concept, I suggest the study of PROCESS THEOLOGY which developed out of the philosophy of A. N. Whitehead. Interpreters of this concept of the Creator and the creation include Daniel Day Williams, Charles Hartshorne, John Cobb, Schubert Ogdon and Lewis S. Ford. See also a paper presented by Charles Birch, "Nature, God and Humanity" at the WCC Conference on Faith, Science and the Future held at MIT, July 1979.

nature and love on earth and his will or intention for us as human beings. I believe that in the historic *Incarnation* God was working in and through Jesus' life, teaching, death, resurrection and continuing presence with his disciples to show us both his steadfast love and purpose, and also the full potentiality of our own personalities.

5. I believe that I live and move and have my existence with a significant awareness of God in my discernment of truth and falsehood, beauty and ugliness, right and wrong, and love and hate. Day after day, these discernments are far more than abstractions and become for me utterly real in actual events and human lives. I see myself in these situations. In them I also am aware of God, whose prompting I know in my mind, heart, conscience and will. I believe that this is God's nearness to me and his *presence* in my life. This is my connection with the spiritual world which is over all as well as in and through everything.

6. I believe that I see this awareness of God as the presence and work of the Holy Spirit. Through my awareness of him I am not given quick and easy answers to complex questions, problems and issues. Rather I am directed to use my intelligence and integrity to work out answers, knowing that as I use the light which I have, more light will come. Moreover the prompting of the Holy Spirit within my consciousness points again and again to the life of Jesus Christ. In this way my Lord and Savior "steps out" of the pages of the New Testament and becomes the guiding and sustaining presence of which I am often aware. My detailed study of Jesus' character — his love, honesty, friendliness, reasonableness, firmness, intolerance, joy, kindness, reverence, holiness, etc. — has become my conscious reference and challenge. Whenever I want to know what any of these elements of character are at their finest, I discover the answer in his life and ministry. Always I must use my intelligence and come to my own decisions but the reference to HIM is, to quite a degree, objective and immeasurably helpful.

7. I believe that the Biblical revelation is *progressive* from the earliest writings in the Old Testament through the New Testament into the teaching and ministry of Christ. This is clearly to be seen in the development of the great themes such as the concepts of God, Man, Social Organization, Right and Wrong, Prayer and Worship, Life After Death, etc. Further I believe that although we see Jesus in the New Testament primarily through

the eyes, hearts and lives of his disciples there are differences between his teachings and those of the Apostles. In so far as these may be discerned through the study of the Gospels, we should choose to follow him.

8. I believe that Christian ethics is epitomized in the commandment, *"Thou shalt love thy neighbor as thyself"* and that the other half of the equation is *"Thou shalt love the Lord thy God with all thy heart, soul, mind and strength."* (Matthew 22:37-40) The essence of Christian ethics is love (*agape*) which requires personal involvement in efforts to achieve justice for individuals as well as social justice. I believe that the words, "I believe" involve much more than intellectual agreement with a concept and that they lay upon us ways to act which, at times, may be quite costly. I believe that Christian love is not so much *what we feel* as *what we do*.

9. I believe in disciplined times of prayer and corporate worship. Time and again I must clarify, renew and deepen my spiritual perceptions so that they do not become subjective, cloudy and self-serving. I believe that this is a danger in all our lives. Nevertheless I find many spontaneous and informal "little prayers" for guidance and strength throughout the day to be not only helpful but also experiences in which the Lord is near and real. The One to whom I pray comforts, rebukes, encourages, judges, gives hope and peace of mind and keeps me going. With Paul I can say "We know that *in everything* God works for good with those who love him, who are called according to his purpose." (Romans 8:28) I too can say, "I know whom I have believed" (2 Timothy 1:12) and "I press on toward the goal for the prize of the upward call of God in Christ Jesus." (Philippians 3:14)

10. I believe that a local church, regarded as merely another among the many social clubs and service organizations in a community is *not* the church at all. So conceived, a person may give it only very marginal interest and support, or pass it by altogether. However, a local church when recognized as part of the Body of Christ (the Discipleship) is an altogether different matter. It is then recognized as a divine as well as a human organization. Its message and work are not of men's choosing but of divine command. (Matthew 28:19, 20)

I believe that a local church, as part of the whole Church, may become one of the world's most creative associations — both for individuals and for society — provided that it:

a. Has a truly great and honest comprehension of Jesus Christ;
   b. Lives under a sense of urgent mission to all people;
   c. Meets human needs directly and indirectly through courageous and sacrificial service; and
   d. Experiences the power of the living Lord in its prayerfully made commitments, corporate worship and outreach in ministering to human needs.

11. I believe that sin is an offense against God's intention for our lives and becomes *my sin* when I deliberately choose my own way in disobedience to his way. When we pray "forgive us . . . as we forgive" we are not asking a human judge to acquit us or to put us on probation. We are not plea-bargaining for special privilege, a reduced sentence, or a pardon. Rather we come to our Heavenly Father asking for forgiveness as his children, and because he loves us. It is as simple and yet as profound as this! Nowhere else do we see more clearly how personal our relationship with God is meant to be, and how redeeming and transforming it may become.

I believe that I need to confess my sin (and particular sins) along with other Christians in corporate worship, as well as in my private prayer life; and I believe that I may be assured of his forgiveness, renewal and saving grace through Jesus Christ, my Lord and Savior.

12. I believe that reference to a personal life beyond this life is necessary to fill out the whole Christian perspective. It is essential for an acceptance of belief in God's justice and love. I believe that he calls me to live to the full here and now investing my time, talents, love and influence — all that I have and all that I am — for his glory in human service. I must pray and work for his Kingdom on earth and when my own physical death comes, I believe that I shall have a place in his transcendent spiritual Kingdom.

I BELIEVE THAT FOR THIS, CHRIST SEEKS TO LAY HOLD OF EVERY ONE OF US!

The Liberating Connection

Read: Matthew 11:28-30

In their carpenter's shop in Nazareth, it is very unlikely that Joseph and Jesus ever made a cross upon which a man might be crucified. It is only Jesus' own death on this instrument of torture and death that changed the cross into a symbol of victory for faith, hope and love. Joseph and Jesus did not make crosses, but it is quite likely that they did make yokes.

In ancient Palestine, oxen and other animals, which were used in ploughing, were united to one another, and to the shaft of the plough, by a yoke. The yoke was a framework of wood, or wood and leather, which joined the two draft animals at their necks.

Jesus made use of the concept of the yoke and so should we.

People Are Yoked Together

People are yoked together in innumerable ways and relationships; husbands and wives; parents and children; teachers and pupils; management and labor; business and professional associates; citizens in a city, state and nation; and through international agreements and organizations. In sacred covenant commitment, members of Christ's Church are yoked together, and with Him.

In all these relationships, much of the satisfaction and happiness in life depends upon how well the yokes fit and are accepted. They may become *liberating connections* or the very opposite.

Being humane men, it seems likely that Joseph and Jesus were aware of the unnecessary pain which even draft animals suffered if the yokes were carelessly designed or poorly made. They may have had this in mind as they did their work. In any case, Jesus made use of the yoke as an important symbol. He showed that yokes may be made of truth and goodwill — and even love — so that those who wear them are able to divide and share burdens and responsibilities helpfully and successfully. Rightly thought of, a yoke is a kind of tool, a means of multiplying strength and influence. All of us are, of necessity, yoked with many others, but if the yokes we wear are fashioned with understanding, mutual respect and helpfulness, they become instruments, not of servitude and torture, but of liberation and blessing.

Many times we ask the question: How may the burdens of life be carried without breaking under the load? One important answer is: through the yoke which we may or must share. Those who do not accept such restraints will go off pulling in opposite directions which can only result in great tensions and ultimate disaster. Many foolishly choose this course. Christ offers something better — *a yoke lined with love.*

It happened a number of years ago. A clergyman who was a passenger on a train observed a young man who was attracting the attention of the other passengers because he seemed unable to sit in one place very long. He was extremely fidgety. At length the pastor went and sat down beside him and said, "What is troubling you? Maybe I can help. I am a minister, and if you feel like telling me, I would like nothing better than to help you if I can."

After a few minutes, the young man said, "You see, Sir, it is like this. In ten or fifteen minutes we will come to my home town; that is, it used to be. Three years ago, I had a terrible quarrel with my father. I said, 'You will never see me again.' I ran away from home. Three years have passed and they have been tough years. Sometimes I wrote my mother. I wrote her last week and told her that I would be on this train passing through. I told her that I would like to come home just once; and I asked her that if it were all right for me to stop, to hang something white outside the house, so that I would know that father had agreed to let me stop. I asked her not to do it unless father wanted it. I had to know how Dad feels."

The young man looked out the window. Suddenly he said to the minister, "Sir, my house is just around the bend, beyond the little hill. Please look for me and see if there is something white?

... If there isn't anything white ... You look, please!" The train lurched a bit as it went around the curve. The minister looked out the window. Then suddenly, grabbing the boy by the arm, he almost shouted, "Look, son, look!" There stood the little house under the trees, but you could hardly see it for the white. It seemed that that father and mother had taken every bed sheet, bedspread, tablecloth, pillowcase, and even handkerchief in the house and had hung them out on the clothesline and trees. The boy's face paled. His lips quivered. He could not talk. His nervous fingers clutched the cheap suitcase he was carrying, and he was off the train as it stopped. The last the passengers on that train saw of him, he was running as fast as his legs would carry him up the hill to the little house where the white things fluttered in the wind.

Some will say that such a story is too sentimental for today. Parents and their sons and daughters are not supposed to love one another — and forgive one another — like this. But in these days we need very much to stop and think. If there were more love in our hearts and more real concern for one another, and a deeper desire for understanding and reconciliation, there would be fewer family tragedies and fewer unhappy and broken individuals. There are now many teenage boys and girls who are lost in our cities and are exploited by the most immoral and criminal elements in our society, while back home many sorrowing fathers and mothers wait and wait for that hot-line call that may never come.

In the midst of human tragedy, the wonderful truth is that God loves us and forgives us, and the knowledge of this has come into our minds and hearts most vividly because Jesus Christ lived on this earth. It is through him that we learn the *Yokefellow Relationship* which is so essential in our relationship with the members of our family, and many others.

Yokes Must Be Accepted

Yokes, if they are to be liberating, must be carefully constructed and honestly accepted.

We now are hearing more and more about the "return to basics" in our schools. And it is about time! Such basics include elementary academic disciplines and the development of respect for the rights of others. Learning is greatly inhibited in any school room where teachers and pupils are at odds. Authority and discipline need to be both fair and firm, and based upon mutual respect. Shouting matches are no more seemly and productive in the classroom than they are in legislative bodies or on the streets. Simple integrity is the essential ingredient needed by all who teach and learn.

Many young people, as well as their parents and teachers, and the general public are realizing that automatic advancement of children through the grades, whether or not they learn anything, is sheer folly. This kind of irresponsibility leads to loss of self-respect, deep frustration and, of course, very inadequate preparation for life. The yoke of a proper educational discipline is the liberating connection between teachers and pupils which results in worthwhile achievement.

The same thing is true of marriage. Many in the "now" generation want everything with little preparation and no waiting: a career, companionship, sex, money and success! They choose to remain single and take life as it comes. They don't want to be committed or to become deeply involved. Many choose to skim along on the surface of life and never know its precious dimensions of a deep and abiding love between husbands and wives, parents and children and family honor and integrity. In the providence of God, marriage is designed to become a very liberating connection, yoking a man and a woman together for life in deep and true love.

Both married and single people need yoked relationships with others. Most of us will not do our best unless we are in tandem with like-minded people, sharing the same principles and pursuing the same objectives and goals. In the arts, the world of business and industry, the professions, government, sports, etc. we should try to find those of like mind, interest and achievement. As we team up with them, our own commitment to integrity and human service is strengthened and enlarged. The making of money should never be the bottom line of our contract with life. In the long run, the making of money, however much may be amassed, costs too much in what it takes from us and others, if it does not contribute to our character and to the good of others.

In the recent past especially, American industry has been seriously weakened by the drive for excessive profits and wages. Both management and labor have been narrowly seeking and getting immediate gains. Neither has cared about the other, or even the future. In the intense battle the slogan of both sides has become "me first, now and always!" On the one hand, workers have been laid off or discharged without concern for them or their families. On the other, the solvency of the company and even its continuation has seemed to be of no concern to the workers: they want simply to be sure that wages go higher and higher, and that there are more fringe benefits. Only now, under the great stress of a widespread recession, have the attitudes of both become more reasonable. Both are yoked and what is made of it determines whether it is a liberating connection or a disaster for all.

As we move into the mid-eighties we, in the United States, are thankful and encouraged over signs of economic recovery in several basic industries. However, proxy wars have shaken the management of some of our best known companies and have cast a shadow over the credibility and solvency of these enterprises. In addition, there is a vast multitude of unemployed, underemployed and hurting people scattered over America in our great cities, small towns and rural areas. On an international level, the economic recycling problem between all countries, and especially those highly industrialized and those which are not, has become serious. Poverty and hunger in the Third World have grown far worse during the last decade. The enormous debt owed by the poorer nations to the financial institutions and governments of the richer nations undermines the security of, and threatens the future of, both. The resulting disarray of people and nations is reflected in the United Nations, and renders relatively ineffective this international organization, designed for peace-making, so desperately needed in this nuclear age.

The nations of this planet, led by the United States and the Soviet Union, are moving toward the incomparable disaster of a nuclear exchange from which there can be no return! If no significant results are achieved in the nuclear arms race, an impasse of enormous seriousness will confront humankind. We are all yoked together in this issue. And the issue is the *power to destroy, and that absolutely vs. the power to survive*. The power to destroy is physical. The power to survive is not physical but is in the rational, moral and spiritual control of the potential firestorm which could envelop the earth.

At this point, our hope can only be in God and what he enables clear-thinking and courageous people to do.

Come Unto Me

To those in every century, and now to us, come the words of Jesus Christ, "Come unto me, all ye that labor and are heavy laden, and I will give you rest. Take my yoke upon you, and learn of me . . ." The quick and superficial reaction of many today is, "What could be less relevant!" But considering the state of the world, and our human condition in it, should we not turn to Christ and learn anew of what he offers?

There is a paradox in the Christian life. Jesus said, "Come unto me, all ye that labor and are heavy laden, and I will give you rest." Many times in our lives we are in a mood to say, "Ah, this is what I need!" How much, in our stress and anguish, we all need comforting! How much we want to escape from all the evils, cares and dangers! But immediately the words come, "Take my yoke upon you, and learn of me." We remember the kind of life he lived and the death he died! We begin to see more deeply that in the life and teaching of Jesus, the call to come and be comforted and the call to come and be responsible in discipleship are hard joined. Only then comes the promise, "Take my yoke upon you, and learn of me . . . and you shall find rest unto your souls, for my yoke is easy, and my burden is light." And, as incredible as it may at first seem, it is dependable!

In order to have God's blessing, we must acknowledge the yoke we share with others. The sublimation of one's own burden of sorrow and suffering through greater dedication to God and to our own families, friends, associates and even strangers along the way, *does* give new strength, new hope and peace of mind and soul. In both the CROSS and the YOKE, Jesus took ideas which must have been revolting to many of his hearers, and gave them new meaning, weaving them into a powerful gospel of hope and peace.

There is another and still more wonderful aspect of the promise which Christians find in Christ's great invitation. When he said, "My yoke," he did not merely refer to the one about which he taught but also the one he was willing and able to share with each of us. And this is the great *liberating connection.* If we attempt to carry the loads of life alone, we may well become overwhelmed. But this need not happen. Christ is the great burden-bearer of all humanity. He is willing to be our YOKE-FELLOW. And with his help, we are able to endure that which, without him, would be impossible. *He provides us, not with a way out of, or escape from, our difficulties, but with the way through them!* It is only possible to experience and understand this as we become aware of a personal one-to-one relationship between ourselves and our Lord.

There is both resource and danger in sensitivity training and encounter groups. It is good, up to a point, to share life with others and to have the strength of friendship and love which honest confrontation may bring about. But frequently, we discover, the exchange of intimate feelings and experiences turns out to have been more spectacular than helpful, and more for effect than for genuine and lasting relationships. Still more serious, such groups have often proceeded without any clear reference to God, and even without deep and true respect for the dignity and integrity of each participant's personhood.

I strongly believe that, beyond a point, no one should lay his or her soul bare to others! Rather, there should be that inner place, that sanctuary in one's own being, which is known only to God. To God, and ultimately to God alone, all of us need to turn, and indeed must turn. I believe that we may help one another best by helping each other turn to God for his healing, and the life he wants us to have. In this, Christ is our Yokefellow and this is the liberating connection we need. Surely this is what St. Paul meant when he exclaimed, "I live, yet not I, but Christ liveth in me." (Galatians 2: 20)

Finally let us apply this truth to the world situation. At times when we think of the problems and disasters which are gravely potential today, we may truly feel overwhelmed, helpless and hopeless. But this is to forget the yoked relationship between ourselves and the eternal God. After all, this is his world and, as always, our hope and our peace of mind are in him.

"Have you not known? Have you not heard? The Lord is the everlasting God, the Creator of the ends of the earth. He does not faint or grow weary . . ." (Isaiah 40:28)

This is the everlasting liberating connection!

FOR THE DISCUSSION GROUP

Outline

I. The "Yoke" as a symbol and concept in human relationships. It may be a liberating connection or the very opposite.
   A. Parents and their children.
   B. God's love and forgiveness.

II. Yokes must be accepted and used.
   A. Teachers and pupils.
   B. "Singles" and "marrieds."
   C. Value-related relationships.
   D. Management and labor.
   E. Economic woes and world tensions.
   F. Power to destroy vs. power to survive in the nuclear age.

III. Christ's invitation (Matthew 11: 28-30).
   A. Irrelevant or on target?
   B. The paradox in the Christian life.
   C. The deeper meaning of "My Yoke."
   D. CHRIST — at the very center of our personal lives.
   E. THE EVERLASTING LIBERATING CONNECTION!

For Discussion

I. Is the "Yoke" an enlightening and motivating symbol for today? Why would it be unacceptable to many? What are its limitations? Compare it with the "Cross" as a Christian symbol. (See sermon-essay No. 15, page 103)

II. Yokes need to be carefully constructed and used.
   A. Why do husbands and wives, parents and children "fight"? How important is "forgiveness" for conflict resolution?
   B. How important are public schools? How do we work for a return to excellence? How may morality and ethics be taught? Is regularly-scheduled *voluntary* prayer possible? Is it really appropriate or necessary in public schools?
   C. Should Money be the bottom line in our "contract" with life?

D. Discuss the economic dilemmas confronting all nations.
E. Will there be a nuclear war? How soon? Who will survive? What must be done in this crisis?

III. The Yoke as a symbol of hope and strength.
A. Are we experiencing Christ as our YOKEFELLOW?
B. What does it mean to put our ultimate trust in the eternal God?

From the Known Into the Unknown

Read: Acts 28

Humankind in the Twentieth Century . . .

No one word can describe it. Perhaps the one which comes closest is AWESOME. Some of us have lived through the First World War, the Great Depression of the thirties and the Second World War in the forties. Then came war in Korea and Vietnam, and turmoil in the Middle East, Africa and Latin America accompanied by appalling conditions of unconscionable wealth and poverty which continue right down to today. Developments in the Soviet Union, China and India have been no less awesome.

We are thankful that our country has not been engaged in a declared war since 1975. Nevertheless military invasion, bloodshed and terrorism continue within and between nations over wide areas of the earth.

Political and economic developments of vast significance continue to follow hard upon one another.

Scientific achievements are incredible and make for both unprecedented weal and woe.

New and far-reaching living patterns between men and women, husbands and wives, parents and children have come seemingly overnight.

Old beliefs have been challenged by new knowledge but, for many, fundamentalism or skepticism have led only to the acceptance of dogmatism.

What mixed feelings of wonder, fear and hope we share day

after day! How can we find our way? How *can* we; how *should* we now live in the '80s?

For the people of England, and everywhere else, Christmas in 1939 was full of anguished foreboding. What should the King say in his annual message? King George VI, in a radio broadcast to the Empire, quoted Minnie Louise Haskins' words:

"And I said to the man who stood at the gate of the year: 'Give me a light that I may tread safely into the unknown.' And he replied: "Go out into the darkness and put your hand into the hand of God. That is to you better and safer than a known way.' "

Is it possible to press forward in the 1980s, with hope and courage, by "placing our hand in the hand of God"? What meaning do such words really have? Is it possible to move from the *known* — for example, our experience of the Providence of God — into the *unknown?*

From the Unknown into the Unknown

For many people today, the situation is quite different and may be described as moving from the unknown, where everything seems confused and nothing is established, into the future which is also unknown, and may be likened only to a big question mark! Many feel that we cannot be sure of anything and that there is no firm ground anywhere. No one can build his house on the rock because there is no rock; all about us is only sand, blowing and shifting in the gale.

This is, of course, a very frightening situation, but many people try to cover up their confusion and uneasiness by suggesting that it is good that nothing is certain. They try to make themselves believe that venturing into the *unknown from the unknown* is not only more exciting but also more courageous. Of course, it is nothing of the sort! They go with blindfolds over their eyes into exploitive sex, into alcoholism and other drug addiction and into various types of criminal activity, excusing themselves with a silly fatalism that says "what will be, will be!" Such foolishness is all too widespread today.

From the Known into the Unknown

A far better way of looking at life, and living it, is to go intelligently from the *known* into the *unknown.* This is the way science and technology move, and must move. Scientific knowledge is obtained by the study and application of what is already known. Systematized knowledge in any field of learning enables the investigators, the researchers and the explorers to go on from what is already known to what there is yet to know. This is the process of moving from the known to the probable but still incomplete, and so develop a body of truth. In this no one needs to start at the beginning; they may, and indeed they must, build upon what others have learned. Young people especially need to see this.

Applied science and technology, whether in agriculture, industry, medicine and surgery or the exploration of outer space, go forward on this basis. Every time orbiting satellites with scientific instruments or human beings are rocketed far beyond the earth, and into very different and hostile physical environments, the basic assumption remains the same: this is a universe where scientific laws and principles are the same and can be depended upon for the success of the experiment, and for life itself.

Another illustration of going from the known into the unknown, and one which is much more familiar to most of us, is our personal travel experience. If, for example, we travel from Lincoln, Nebraska, to Chicago, to Detroit, through Canada to Niagara Falls, and then on to New York City, we need good road maps. Such maps represent the known — that is, what has previously been discovered, accomplished and recorded. However, as we travel anywhere, there are many unknowns along the way and *many life-determining decisions to be made!* Regardless of how many millions have traveled these roads before us, our journey becomes very much *our* journey.

In 1961 Mrs. Roblee and I went to Japan for a summer time mission in Christian evangelism. Although we went with other Americans and Canadians, and all of us were briefed in Tokyo, we were asked to serve in a community where we would be the only non-Japanese, and where there was only one small Christian church. I still remember my feelings as we flew toward that strange oriental country, and as our big plane circled over Tokyo. In many ways, we discovered Japan to be a different world. In more ways, however, it is very much like ours. What a different outlook on life! What new experiences! And what fine new Christian friendships we made, many of which continue to this day. With previous experience, and our Christian knowledge and faith to guide us, we moved from the known into the Japanese unknown, and good came from it.

Experience and Faith

The wonderful truth is that we may have road maps, great travel experiences, and, if we will, sustaining faith as we move into the unknown tomorrow. Was it not of this that King George VI of England spoke when he told his countrymen at the beginning of the terrrible Second World War, "Go out into the darkness and put your hand in the hand of God"?

Some people, hearing such a sermon as this, would say, "You give us a much too rosy picture of life. Life isn't that sweet or easy." Certainly, life isn't easy, nor is it all good. Rather, life is like an obstacle course. All along the way, there are great dangers and difficulties, great sorrows and disappointments, and much loneliness and many times of despair. Along with our personal and family distresses there are wars, Watergates, poverty, racism, inflation, recession and incredible examples of our inhumanity to one another!

Can our faith withstand such great shaking? Can we still believe in the God about whom Jesus spoke, and then press on? Can we keep our personal integrity and our commitment to help others? It isn't easy, but it is possible, and it is what, with God's help, we must do. We must think of *divine providence* — not as God's predetermination of all that will ever happen to us, but rather as God's presence and help. We need to count on God's availability in our lives at every crucial turn, and in the final outcome.

There is much that indicates that family life, as we have known and cherished it in America, is coming apart at the seams. Television, radio, the theater, novels and magazines unashamedly portray every sex aberration, including promiscuity, mate-swapping, prostitution and homosexuality. How can anyone live decently in such an age? How can marriage, creative parenthood and Christian family life grow in such unholy ground? It isn't easy! But when has it ever been easy to be a Christian, or even a decent person?

In these days we must stand up for what we know to be right. We must use our intelligence and have personal integrity. We need to see that much of what is being called the "new morality" is nothing more than the "old immorality" that has always led to much tragedy. We must reverse the disintegration of our society, and even our churches, by first taking firm personal stands for self-respect, and then respect for *the person* of every other man, woman or child. We need to do this in reverence for God, our Creator, and for our fellow human beings whom he has placed upon the earth.

There are many fine contemporary illustrations of victorious faith, but those found in Scripture speak just as loudly. Toward the end of his most remarkable career, in his address before King Agrippa — and when his life hung in the balance — Paul declared, *"I was not disobedient to the heavenly vision."* This is what made Paul the person he was and kept him going. For him, the "heavenly vision" had profound implications for the life to come beyond this world, but it was not limited to that ultimate assurance. It enabled him to be the great Apostle to the Gentiles and so help, in the Providence of God, to launch the Church on its ageless mission to all humanity. It powered him for the life he was then living in the present, real world.

In this mission we still share, and for its furtherance, we have great responsibility. Our responsibility begins right here in our own church but it also extends out, and out, and out — from the known into the unknown! *For us, Christ and his influence upon us and countless others is the great unknown.* There is a beautiful and powerful reminder of this in the recurrence of Christmas just before the beginning of each new year. In living faith, we may put our hand in the hand of God, and go forth!

FOR THE DISCUSSION GROUP

Outline

I. Looking at the twentieth century.
   A. World Wars and now A-bombs.
   B. Unconscionable wealth and poverty.
   C. Far-reaching political and economic developments.
   D. Incredible scientific achievements.
   E. New living patterns.
   F. Dogmatism.

II. How *can* we — how *should* we — live in the '80s?
   A. "Putting our hand in the hand of God." Providence as the "known."
   B. From the unknown into the unknown.
   C. From the known into the unknown future.

III. Experience and faith.
   A. Personal experiences which illustrate a trusting life.
   B. St. Paul's "I was not disobedient to the heavenly vision."
   C. Our responsibility to know Christ and our witness for him.

For Discussion

I. "Awesome."
   A. Is the list too optimistic or pessimistic?
   B. What other items should be listed? Should any be deleted?
   C. What about modern science: For weal? Or woe?
   D. What is happening to the family as the basic "building block" of society? Gains and losses for women? men? children?
   E. Do we really want the truth?

II. "Putting our hand into the hand of God."
   A. Is this a good understanding of Providence?
   B. Does moving "from the unknown into the unknown" describe our times?
   C. "From the Known into the Unknown": can this proven procedure apply to trusting God?

III. "Our journey" remains "*our* journey."
   A. List other examples of a trusting life.
   B. List others in the Bible, besides St. Paul, who trusted. Compare them with those listed above.
   C. How may our responsibility to witness add to our personal experience?

The Road, Through Doubt, to Faith

Read: John 1:43-46 and Matthew 7:7-8; 13-21

For some people, there may be a road to faith which does not pass through the valley of doubt. However, we must not suppose that this is the only road or even the one which is most commonly traveled. The truth is that most people who arrive at a sturdy and really vital personal faith have passed through dark and discouraging experiences. When we study our Bibles, we find many illustrations of this. Let us therefore, in this sermon, take a good look at the road, through doubt, to faith for many walk and must walk upon it before they are able to achieve a strong and enduring faith in God, in themselves and in their relations with others.

The Need to Doubt

God did not make this an easy world in which to live. Goethe once said: "What you have inherited from your fathers, you must earn for yourself, before you can call it your own." George MacDonald put it this way: "Each generation must do its own seeking and finding. What the fathers found is only the warrant for the children's search." We have but to recall the struggles for existence, for social progress and for personal character to realize how true this is. As strange as it may seem, most often the road to faith is, and must be, through doubt!

To begin with, we need to remind ourselves that many things, which are not true or are only half-true, must be doubted, for such doubt is essential in the discovery of the real truth. There are many prejudices, ancient and contemporary. Our times have not escaped the plague of many serious half-truths!

For a long time, people believed that the earth was flat and that the sun, moon and stars passed above it. This concept was vigorously and emotionally defended. The belief that the earth was the center of the universe persisted as late as the seventeenth century and Galileo was forced by the Inquisition to renounce his discovery that it was not. The old theories had to be doubted before the real truth could come, and be accepted.

In a parallel way, honest doubt has, for many people, an important place in the development of their conviction about God, Christ and the Christian way of life. Jesus himself was a doubter, a magnificent doubter, of many things that were strongly believed and defended in his generation.

All about him were people who said that the Samaritans were an inferior breed. Jesus dared to doubt that commonly held assumption. He deliberately chose to go through Samaria, rather than around it, as many did; and he mingled with those he met, including women — an unheard of thing for a Jewish teacher to do in those days. In one of his greatest parables he dared to teach that a good Samaritan is far better than an indifferent Jew, even if that one were a priest or Levite!

Again, all about Jesus were people who sought to show that they were religious by making long prayers, wearing broad phylacteries and observing strict laws concerning Sabbath observance and the food to be eaten. Leather cases called phylacteries were worn around the head, and armlets worn around the arms contained words of Scripture. Often such customs were ostentatiously practiced. Jesus doubted the sincerity or value of such exhibits of piety and said so. In their place, he opened the door to a different understanding of the religious life.

Another illustration: Jesus was a daring doubter in his repudiation of the hope and expectation held by many in his day that there would come to Israel a Messiah-King who would rule the world from Jerusalem. Hating their Roman overlords as they did, many hoped and believed fanatically that the Messiah would come with great heavenly and earthly power and would avenge their enemies. Jesus dared to doubt this whole concept of the Messiah and to turn the thoughts of the people to a different teaching found in the Second Isaiah, the great Prophet of the Exile, who said that God's Messiah would come as the Suffering Servant of the Lord. And Jesus not only adopted this as one of the key ideas associated with the Messiah but called his disciples to stand with him and share the spirit and work of God's servant people.

There are, of course, many other illustrations in the ministry and teaching of Jesus, as well as in our own lives which point to the fact that things which are not true, or are only half-true must be doubted, and such doubt is essential for the working out of the real truth. It was a mature Christian who said, "He who never doubted, never half believed." Nothing is so intimate and utterly personal as one's own relationship to God! No one can hand to another a ready-made religious faith. Sturdy faith just doesn't come that easily.

Martin Luther was a man of faith. Indeed, his faith was so strong that he could give the world the powerful hymn, "A Mighty Fortress Is Our God." Yet Luther, many times, had to walk through the valley of doubt. Indeed, had he not done so, he would not have been the great spokesman for the Protestant Reformation! And his doubts, at times, were deeply personal. On one such occasion he said, "For more than a week, Christ was wholly lost. I was shaken by desperation and blasphemy against God."

Dostoyevsky, the great Russian novelist of the last century, said, "It is not like a child that I believe in Christ and confess HIM. My hosanna has come forth from the crucible of doubt."

Few religious leaders have spoken more clearly and helpfully to today's doubters than has Harry Emerson Fosdick. He was able to do this because he himself had known deep-seated and soul-searching doubts. Looking back over his life, he wrote, "When I started for college my junior year, I told my mother that I was going to clear God out of the universe and begin all over to see what I could find. I could not swallow the Christian faith unquestioningly. I had to fight for it. And so it's mine today!"

Doubting Our Doubts

When we study the life of a man like Dr. Fosdick, whose critical and ever searching mind opened avenues of truth to many, we discover another important aspect of the relationship between faith and doubt. We find, as he pointed out, that an honest seeker for truth must frequently doubt his doubts! This is true in the quest for religious belief, and it is also true in all the great and most daring ventures in life.

It was in 1927 that Charles A. Lindbergh made his solo flight in a light plane across the Atlantic from New York to Paris. That flight opened a whole new era in travel and communication. He flew thirty-six hundred miles in thirty-three hours. That day in May, while he was over the water, I attended my class in geology at Washington University in St. Louis. Everyone was thinking and talking about Lindbergh and his flight. I remember that the Professor of Geology digressed from his lecture that morning to say that he very much doubted that he would make it to Paris. Among the reasons which he advanced for his view was that no propeller could stand such a long continued strain! There were others who, for various reasons, also doubted that Lindbergh would ever make it. Lindbergh had to doubt such doubts, and risk all, before he could prove that a man, all alone in a light plane, could fly across the ocean!

In achieving religious faith and conviction, it is often necessary to doubt our doubts. Let us recall the situation when Jesus was calling his disciples. He began among the disciples of John the Baptizer. According to the Fourth Gospel, Philip was among those to whom Jesus first spoke. Soon thereafter, Philip sought out his friend Nathanael and said to him, "We have found him of whom Moses in the law and also the prophets wrote, Jesus of Nazareth, the son of Joseph." Nathanael was acquainted with Nazareth and was scornful of it. He felt that the Messiah could never come from such a place. Therefore, with cynical disbelief, he said, "Can anything good come out of Nazareth?" Philip did not start an argument. He merely said, "Come and see" — which is a way of saying, "Doubt your doubts, Nathanael!"

In recent years, some youth have vied with one another to see who could come up with the most cynical views of life. They have said such things as: "Life is a bad joke." "Life is a jail sentence which we get for the crime of being born." "Life is a disease for which the only cure is death." Fortunately people — young and old alike — soon get their fill of such nonsense and begin to doubt their doubts! Life simply can't be so cynically conceived for the obvious reason that if it were, the civilization which we have could never have come into existence!

There are two kinds of hypocrites. Some people are hypocrites because they do not live up to what they profess. Others are hypocrites who really believe more and live more than they profess! They belittle and disparage their own integrity, their own faith and good intentions and actions. This too is a kind of hypocrisy and it is deadly. It does nothing to strengthen life but only weakens it. There is deep need to profess and live what we believe, if we are going to hold fast to what we really believe! Jesus spoke of these two kinds of hypocrisy. He denounced sham in no uncertain terms: "Sound no trumpet before you, as the hypocrites do in the synagogues and in the streets, that they may be praised by men." (Matthew 6:2) But he also warned, in no uncertain terms, against appearing in a worse light than we really are — that is, belittling what we really believe and are! He said, "Men do not light a candle, and put it under a bushel, but on a candlestick . . . (Matthew 5:15) Let your light so shine before men, that they may see your good works and give glory to your Father who is in heaven." (Matthew 5:16) We need to show our faith rather than our fear; our courage rather than our cowardice; and our best, not our worst.

A Very Positive Affirmation!

In this way we go beyond "doubting our doubts" and develop a workable faith, and the strength to live! We need to have a passion for the truth and the willingness to stake our lives upon it. Of all people, we Christians, following Christ, should make the truth the basis for all that we say and do. Whether it be in science, religion, politics, or our relationships with others, far from being afraid of the truth, we should be very much afraid of anything less!

Hear again the words of Jesus: "You will know them by their fruits. Are grapes gathered from thorns, or figs from thistles? So, every sound tree bears good fruit, but the bad tree bears evil fruit . . . . Thus you will know them by their fruits." (Matthew 7: 16-20)

Jesus also said, "I am the Way, the Truth, and the Life." (John 14:6) He meant this to be an invitation to discipleship and to learning to live! And so the challenge comes to each one of us. Like Nathanael we have heard the call of Christ's followers, "Come and see." Hopefully we have extended that invitation to others and will continue to do so. Then, across the days of our years we will be able to say with more and more conviction: *He is, indeed, the Way, the Truth, and the Life.*

FOR THE DISCUSSION GROUP

Outline

I. The road through doubt.
   A. For many it is real and necessary.

II. The need to doubt.
   A. Doubting is essential in the discovery of truth.
   B. Jesus was a doubter.
      1. Prejudice against Samaritans.
      2. False piety.
      3. Concept of Israel's expected Messiah-King.
   C. Other famous "doubters."

III. Doubting our doubts.
   A. Daring ventures in life become possible when we learn to doubt our doubts.
   B. Cynical views of life must be rejected.
   C. Two kinds of hypocrites.
   D. Living up to what we believe.

IV. Positive affirmation.
   A. A passion for the truth is needed.
   B. "You will know them by their fruits."
   C. The invitation to discipleship.

For Discussion

I. Faith and doubt.
   A. Do we know of some who lost their faith because of unanswered doubts?
   B. Has our own faith been strengthened because we met and handled our doubts?

II. Dogmatism.
   A. How do we react to dogmatism?
   B. Do we applaud such positions if they agree with our opinions?
   C. Discuss the "roots" of some common prejudices. Are prejudices ever good? If so — why? how?

III. Authority.
   A. Does a person's position necessarily make him or her an

authority? A police officer? A judge on the bench? A scientist in his laboratory? Discuss appeal to "higher" authority.
- B. How may we wisely "doubt our doubts"? Are the achievements worth the risk?
- C. In all of us there are both kinds of hypocrisy. Into which type are we most likely to fall?

IV. Passion for truth.
- A. Jesus gave a pragmatic test when he said, "You will know them by their fruits." But what fruits? For whom? Can such a test become valid for a Christian except in the context of Christ's life and teaching?
- B. Will passion for the truth make us strong?
- C. What has this to do with discipleship?

God Has a Plan for Our Lives

Read: Genesis 45:1-8 and John 15:10-17

Horace Bushnell was one of the most famous ministers and civic leaders of the nineteenth century. He had a profound influence on the religious and cultural life of New England. In what was perhaps his best known sermon, entitled "Every Man's Life a Plan of God," this preacher declared, "God has a definite lifeplan for every human person, girding him, visibly and invisibly, for some exact thing, which it will be the true significance and glory of his life to have accomplished." This is a fascinating idea and a powerful one, but it needs careful interpretation. There are problems with it.

A few years ago, we received a letter from a friend in her nineties. She was one of three members of the Pastor Nominating Committee which came to St. Louis from Bay City, Michigan, many years ago to take a look at me and see if I might be the one to become the pastor of the First Presbyterian Church. All through our fifteen years in that church, we were very good friends, and I have never known a more alert and delightful person. In this letter she wrote, "I broke my right leg, upon leaving a friend's car, on my way to our church. The following Saturday my granddaughter was married in Midland. I could not attend. I received a letter from my cousin in which she said, 'It is too bad you could not go to your granddaughter's wedding but God did not wish you to attend that wedding, and so your leg was broken.' I was so astonished and really angry to have this interpretation of my accident that I haven't answered this strange letter." Surely we have here, in this cousin's letter, a serious misunderstanding of God's will for each person.

On a deeper level, we need to clarify our thinking. Is it possible to believe that God has a plan for every one of us while such things as the birth of deformed children, the inexpressible horrors of warfare, tragic injustice and blind suffering are all about us? If God is in absolute control of everything it is impossible to believe that he is a loving Heavenly Father. As one sensitive person put it, "Your 'God' is my devil"! Must we conclude, then, that there is no God or, if there is, that he has no love, no interest or concern for individuals? In this sermon, we cannot say everything that needs to be said about such an all-inclusive subject, but let us make a start.

What Does It Mean, "God Has a Plan . . ."?

What does it mean to say that God has a plan for your life and mine? A "plan" is a proposal, a working outline, a hope; it is not something already finally determined. It is not an unalterable blueprint. It is not a fixed calendar of events which must take place as scheduled. Even plans as minutely worked out as were those designed to send men to the moon and return them to earth were subject to change, and highly important new decisions were made as each step of the great adventure was taken. This, I believe, is true of God's plan for each one of us.

Human parents cannot and do not control everything in the heredity, environment and free choice of their children. If they did, their young people would not be the individuals which they are, nor would they be responsible persons. Wise parents, therefore, have plans for their sons and daughters but do not attempt to regiment their lives. Quite to the contrary, fathers and mothers provide for the development of freedom of choice in their homes and through the participation of their children in schools, churches, camps and many activities. Through it all, parents plan for and hope that their children will achieve self-control which is the essence of freedom and the basis of character. In this they show their love for each son and daughter.

In much the same way, and for the same fundamental reasons, God does not control everything in a person's heredity, environment and free choice, yet he has a plan, a purpose and a great love for each one of us. Let it be clear: *God, the sovereign and eternal Creator, in his infinite wisdom and goodness, has chosen to limit himself by bringing into existence free and responsible human personalities; men and women who may be obedient to his divine plan and intention for them and so achieve* significantly or, who, choosing not to seek and follow his will, suffer the consequences of a selfish and misdirected life.

God Does Care

We should not conclude that God is without love or concern for us because he made the world this way. On the contrary, it is clear that only in this kind of a world, where responsibility is real and personal, can there be moral character, faith, hope and love. God wants us to be his responsible sons and daughters, not his marionettes or slaves. This is the basic Christian truth and it does much to clarify our whole experience. It is simply not true that God controls everything including such things as the birth of deformed children, injustice and suffering. Evil is contrary to God's will and results from the denial of that will. Nevertheless, as St. Paul said so well, *not* "all things work together for good" but "*In everything God works for good with those who love him, who are called according to his purpose.*" (Romans 8:28 RSV)

A number of years ago, a true story appeared in the *Reader's Digest* which helps us to get our thinking straight about the nature of God's providence. It was written by a mother whose son was crippled by polio at age five. She and her husband wanted for their boy a full and valuable life. But how could this be? She wrote: "We told each other that to do this he must give all he could to the world, rather than take all that people rushed to hand him." This was both difficult and painful to accomplish. There was the struggle just to preserve life. Then there were two apparently fruitless operations. There were times when the little crippled boy didn't want to study, so there were occasions when he got spanked. Later his courageous parents encouraged him to play baseball. All along there were painful treatments which simply had to be endured. When he was in high school, one of his fellow-students became very sick and needed a transfusion. His parents suggested that he give some of his blood, and he did. Still later another daring operation seemed indicated and he underwent it. At the time the article was written, he was studying to become an orthopedic surgeon! These parents were both kind and unusually wise with their son. Although they could not and did not prevent polio from striking him down at five years of age, and although they could not control many other harmful or painful experiences, nevertheless they had a plan, a purpose and a great and wise love for him.

The Christian concept of divine providence is not the idea of some kind of supernatural manipulation of all human affairs.

Rather it is the profound and wonderful truth of the dynamic love, the dynamic Fatherhood, of God. Even as the parents of this crippled boy had a plan which of necessity involved discipline and steadfast purpose and love, so God has a plan, a purpose and love for us.

In perhaps its most awesome dimension, it is the Christian faith, as Horace Bushnell said, that God has a particular life-plan or special accomplishment for each one of us to work out! In this we are not speaking about an earthly parent or parents, but God. What would be both impossible and unwise for us, as quite fallible human parents, is not impossible or unwise for him. And we may, indeed, believe that he wants us to do something for him and for our fellow humans which only we can do! If we fail to do it, the total fabric of God's great design is imperfect and incomplete to just that degree. This awesome truth is suggested in the New Testament and is in the Letter to the Hebrews where it is affirmed that, "Apart from us they (that is those about us) should not be made perfect." (Hebrews 11:40)

Even from our very limited outlook, if we have tried to know and do God's will we come to an awareness that we are being guided. As I come closer to the end of my career, and my life, I have an awareness that something very much like this is true! This is one of the perspectives that comes with advancing years, and with it also the true meaning and glory of our lives. We discover for ourselves what the wise man of old meant when he said, "In all your ways acknowledge him, and he will make straight your paths." (Proverbs 3:6) In this we may believe that as our life develops, favorably or unfavorably, so also does God's plan for us change to the end that the highest possible good may come in and through our existence on earth. This is the profound insight of Process Theology, that God's creativity never stops.

Such Faith Changes Things

Such belief in and first-hand discovery of God's plan for our lives makes a tremendous difference. Living becomes daringly purposeful for good! And great things can and do happen. Horace Bushnell struggled all his life against poor health but, believing that God had a plan for his life, he discovered it and really made his life count. Helen Keller, although blind and deaf from the age of two, discovered God's will for her life and made it glorious. She said, "I like to think that through my limitations God is working out some good purpose. My troubles have also been great adventures. They have brought me understanding, friendship and taught me how to serve the world." Here, in the words of Helen Keller, is the secret of true greatness and peace of mind.

The tragedy in so many lives is that there is no belief in any such divine plan. Often, instead, people accept a blind fatalism and then compound the error by attributing that to God and calling it the Christian Faith. Exactly the opposite is true. What we have been talking about this morning is not fatalism but God's love and purpose at work in our lives. If and when such belief is ours, the outlook on everything changes. We gain a different perspective and we place quite different values on things. We are no longer so much concerned about what we have, as what we are becoming. We are no longer willing to sacrifice the things which matter most for the things which matter least. And our own lives are given a new dignity and worth.

One of the finest teachers I ever had was Andrew C. Zenos who, for many years, was the Dean of McCormick Theological Seminary in Chicago. He had a remarkable way of teaching. Clearly he wanted for every one of his students a sound theological education, and a good ministry in the church. In class, whenever a student made an incorrect answer, no matter how foolish it was, Dean Zenos found something good about it before going on to explain the right answer. In his relation with us, God is like this. Keeping always in mind the objective of a good and useful life for us to choose and follow, the Lord redirects his guidance of our life toward modified goals and disciplines. This is not really to change his "plan" for our lives but to bring it to pass, if only, we will respond and do our part. God is our great Teacher!

Have you ever wondered what it was that enabled a handful of Jesus' first disciples, amid tremendous problems and hostilities, to change the world? Well, they had a wonderful story to tell. That much is true. But beyond that, they were commissioned people! They had been given a great job to do, a personal mission to accomplish. They had heard Jesus say, "You did not choose me, but I chose you and appointed you." (John 15:16) And they accepted that appointment!

The biggest factor in youth guidance is somehow to say effectively, "God has a plan and a purpose for your life — he really has — and there are ways you can discover that plan and fulfill it." Christian parents, and other older Christians, need to teach young people that the finest secret of life lies in this discovery. Then having told them, they must help youth understand by demonstrating, across the years, that God's plan is working out in their own lives.

FOR THE DISCUSSION GROUP

Outline

I. "Every man's life a plan of God."
   A. A fascinating and powerful idea, but there are problems.
   B. Serious misunderstanding concerning God's will. An illustration.
   C. "Your 'God' is my devil"!

II. What does it mean, "God has a plan . . . "?
   A. A "plan" is not something finally determined.
   B. Human parents don't control everything in their children's lives.
   C. God's self-limitation in the creation of human beings.

III. God does care.
   A. Only in this kind of world can moral character, faith, hope and love develop. An illustration.
   B. The dynamic Fatherhood of God.

IV. Such belief changes things.
   A. Living becomes daringly purposeful and good. Illustrations.
   B. Not fatalism but God's love and purpose.
   C. God — our great Teacher. An illustration.

V. The strength of Jesus' disciples in changing the world.
   A. "I chose you."
   B. Our example important in youth guidance.

For Discussion

I. The dilemma.
   A. Do we know anyone like this elderly woman's cousin? How would we react to such a letter?
   B. In view of all the evil and suffering in the world is "Your 'God' is my devil" too strong a reaction? Can God possibly be our "Heavenly Father"?

II. Human choice.
   A. How important is human choice? Could we be human without it?
   B. How many parents plan for their child's freedom and ability to choose wisely?
   C. Are parents entirely responsible when things go wrong?
   D. Study carefully the statement about God's self-limitation in order that human beings may choose for themselves.

III. Do we want to be free?
   A. Freedom of choice involves very much more than we may at first think. Do we really want it?
   B. Many would rather be controlled by others, but this *is* a choice and often a very sad one. Give examples.
   C. Can we — *must* we — believe that God has a particular life-plan for each of us to work out?

IV. What about guidance?
   A. We all have stood at many crossroads of decision. Do we feel that we have had divine guidance? If so, has this come about with our willingness to respond?
   B. Do we feel that the Lord has had a part in re-directing our lives toward modified goals?
   C. Are prayer and guidance a part of our daily life?

V. Power in discipleship.
   A. In this difficult and dangerous time, can we find the courage and strength to do God's will?
   B. Do we feel that we have been commissioned?
   C. What kind of Christian witness are we making, especially with youth?

Bible — Word and Spirit
Read: Matthew 5:13-24 and Hebrews 4:12

One Sunday, Joseph Fort Newton, a famous pastor of City Temple Church in London, told his congregation of a dream which he had had. He had dreamed, he said, that one day England had awakened to find that the Bible was gone, not only the book but also its influence. The results were appalling. Great literature became unintelligible. Shakespeare was beyond comprehension and gorgeous passages from Ruskin looked like moth-eaten tapestry. Even on the street, everyday speech faltered. A great change came over the whole tone and temper of the people. God's name was spoken increasingly without reverence and only in illiterate profanity. Life became hectic, hurried and just plain vulgar. Crime and immorality sharply increased. All values were blurred and people became petty and mean. Everything seemed drab, tedious and trivial!

Was all this mere fiction? Was it only a bad dream? Is the Bible all that important? Is this what has happened, and is still happening, in England and America today? Unquestionably the Bible has profoundly shaped our heritage and our culture, but now? An intelligent understanding and right use of Scripture is essential to the Christian faith and witness. Why don't more people study the Bible and discover it to be the great resource which it really is?

A minister was calling in the home of one of the members of his church. As he and his parishioner were visiting he asked for a copy of the Bible that he might read it to her. She called her little daughter, who was in the next room, to run and get "that book which we all love." Soon the little girl returned and handed her mother the latest copy of the Sears Roebuck Catalogue! Material things — buying and selling — have crowded out almost everything else in our lives.

What Turns People Off

In today's world, there are many things that turn people away from the Bible. Let us name some of them.

Many people, if they open a Bible at all, simply do not know what to make of it. They find between its covers many little books, sixty-six in number. These books are not arranged in chronological order. In many cases, the material within a book is arranged neither topically nor chronologically. It is, therefore, necessary to understand that both the Old Testament and the New Testament are anthologies such as we have for English and American literature. To be sure, we consider the Biblical anthologies to be special — they are canonical Scriptures. Nevertheless, they are compilations of many writings.

The books of the Bible were written and compiled over a period of at least 1500 years. They reflect many literary forms: ancient ballads and stories, history, parables, hymns, proverbs, sermons, letters and apocalyptical writings. It should be obvious, therefore, that before we can interpret any passage we must know what kind of literary composition it is.

A good example is the Book of Jonah, best thought of as an Old Testament parable about a prophet who disobeyed God's command. The Lord told him to go and preach to the sinning people of Nineveh but he took a ship to Tarshish, far in the opposite direction. He did this — in part, at least — because he did not like the Ninevites and did not want them to repent and receive God's forgiveness. A great storm came upon the ship, and to save themselves, the sailors cast Jonah into the sea which then quieted. Jonah was swallowed by a great fish. After three days and nights Jonah was spewed out on the seashore. A second time the Lord commanded him to preach to the people of Nineveh. This time he obeyed and the people repented and were saved. However, instead of being glad, Jonah was angry with God.

This parable teaches us at least two lessons. First, when the Lord tells us to do something, we had better do it. On a deeper level, we learn that God's love is for all people, not just for one's own race or nation, as Jonah wanted to believe. In this way, the Book of Jonah is close to the teaching of the New Testament. It is unfortunate that for years some people have debated whether a man could live three days inside a fish! This is to misunderstand the kind of writing in this book, and the real point and message this Old Testament story had, and still has for today.

Another thing that turns people from Scripture is the tendency to regard the Bible as a book of "proof texts." By choosing Bible verses at random and out of context, people can support any position they may wish. This way of using the Bible has led to all kinds of errors and excesses. For example, in the early days of our country some people in New England focused on the words found in Exodus 22:18, "Thou shalt not suffer a witch to live" and put innocent people to death, alleging they were witches! And, not long ago, there was a story in our newspaper about a mother who killed her three-year-old son because she believed that he was bewitched! Race prejudice and slavery were justified by many who quoted Noah's words found in Genesis 9:25, "Cursed be Canaan; a slave of slaves shall he be." This verse had nothing to do with the terrible enslavement of black people in our country, yet was used to justify it! Such use of Scripture, entirely out of historical context and quite contrary to the Biblical message as a whole, has done immeasurable harm. The "proof text" method of interpretation has been and continues to be a leading cause of many unfortunate tensions and divisions in the church.

Here then are some things which "turn people off;" but there is very much in the Bible which can and should "turn them on"!

The Greatness of the Bible

The true greatness of the Bible, and its significance for today and for our own personal needs, may be discovered or rediscovered and enlarged for each one of us. For such a discovery, however, it is necessary to ask and answer such questions as: Who wrote this passage? When was it written? For whom was it written? What was its essential teaching for that time, place and circumstance? Only after such questions are dealt with in some depth and with some integrity is it possible to know how the passage is applicable to present-day personal and social issues! It is exactly such honest searching that often is frowned upon by those who want no questioning of their interpretations. Instead they demand acceptance of their simplistic answers and assertions. Let all such "Bible teachers" take much more seriously Paul's admonition to Timothy, "Do your best to present yourself to God as one approved, a workman who has no need to be ashamed, rightly handling the word of truth." (II Timothy 2:15)

One excellent way to study the Bible and *have it become our teacher* is to study how great themes develop throughout the Old Testament and the New Testament, such as:

The Being and Purpose of God
The Nature and Destiny of Humanity
How to Discern Between Right and Wrong
Social Responsibility
Prayer and Communion With God, and
Sin, Salvation and Eternal Life

These and other subjects await our study and are for our guidance. In the Hebrew and Christian Scriptures they are revealed historically over a vast reach of time, and in many lives. As we pursue such study we learn to have an open mind concerning what a marvelous "resource library" the Bible truly is. And we become eager to let it speak for itself.

In addition to this, we must see the important place which the Bible should have in our Christian experience and witness. Most of all, we need to be receptive to God's living Word for us — both behind and beyond the words of the Bible. This is a Biblically-sound and historically-important theological concept. Phillips Brooks, that beloved pastor of the last century who wrote, "O Little Town of Bethlehem," made clear the difference between seeing the Bible and seeing *through* the Bible to God and his living Word. He said that "the Bible is like a telescope." One may look *at* it and see only a telescope, or one may look *through* it and see the heavens. Before reading the Scriptures in a service of worship, I say to the congregation, "Let us hear the Word of God." By this I mean much more than, "Please pay attention to the words I will read." Beyond this we ministers, who use such an introductory statement, ask all *to listen for what God would say to us* through understanding the passage correctly and applying it. This is also the proper introduction to every sermon. It should likewise be the spoken or implied prayer before any devotional reading of the Bible or study of Scripture.

A great experience of "looking through" the Hebrew Scriptures came to the first Christians when they discovered the *living Word* in the person of Jesus Christ. They heard him say, "Think not that I have come to abolish the law and the prophets; I have come not to abolish them but to fulfill them . . . You have heard that it was said to men of old . . . but I say to you." (Matthew 5:17,22) The impression Jesus made on them was profound and transforming. His disciples went everywhere telling what he had said and done. They wrote it down. Now we read what they wrote and we see him through those who had been with him. And so today, the living Word will become alive in us, and through us for others. Such is the work of the Holy Spirit bearing witness to Christ in the lives of his disciples. (See John 16:12 ff.)

This Great Experience Is for Our Discovery

John Calvin made much of prayer for God's illumination of his Word. And today, a contemporary expression of the Reformed Faith declares that "As God has spoken his word in diverse cultural situations, the church is confident that he will continue to speak through the Scriptures in a changing world and in every form of human culture. God's word is spoken to his church today where the Scriptures are faithfully preached and attentively read in dependence on the illumination of the Holy Spirit and with readiness to receive their truth and direction." (*Book of Confessions*, the Presbyterian Church (U.S.A.) 9:29, 30)

If, therefore, we are to discover the living Word in, through and beyond the words of the Bible we should know what to expect! And what *should* we expect? The writer of the Letter to the Hebrews tells us that "the word of God is living and active, sharper than any two-edged sword . . . discerning the thoughts and intentions of the heart." (Hebrews 4:12)

The Word of God comes to us as a sword! As we read the Bible, we discover that this was so in the lives of Abraham, Jacob, Joseph, Moses, David, Amos, Isaiah, Jeremiah and Peter, John, Mark, Paul, Luke and many others. None of them were "ready-made saints" but mortals like ourselves who struggled between good and evil. As God worked with them so he will work with us; as they responded, so may we!

We need to learn to read the Bible as adults should, that is, much more realistically. The Bible does not present a "sugar-coated" religion or view of the world — far from it! In a world like this today, the Word of God is and must be a sword in the conscience. Only as we feel the pain, and respond out of a sorely troubled conscience is there hope.

The poor, the starving, the outcast, the boat people, and the oppressed and rejected everywhere need liberation. Yes, and the Word of God tells the rest of us that *we also need liberation* — liberation from fear and greed, from too many possessions, from the misuse of power and wealth, and from the cancer of selfishness.

The Word of God comes to us as a sword; but it also comes to us with divine comfort and reassurance. Only Christ has the sure word of forgiveness and renewal, of hope and eternal life. He speaks with authority about the things which really matter now, and for the future. Thus for untold numbers of people, behind the words of the Bible stands Christ. This is the true and abiding greatness of the Bible. For those who read, understand and give their lives to him, Christ becomes the center of time and eternity.

FOR THE DISCUSSION GROUP

Outline

I. Newton's dream.
   A. The Bible has profoundly shaped our heritage of faith and culture.

II. What turns people off.
   A. The unusual nature of the Book.
   B. The many literary forms found in the Old Testament and New Testament.
   C. The "proof text" method of interpretation.

III. The greatness of the Bible.
   A. Questions that must be answered.
   B. The study of great themes developing through the Old Testament and New Testament.
   C. God's "living Word" behind the words.

IV. The work of the Holy Spirit.
   A. Spoken to the church in an ever changing world.
   B. Comes to us as a "sword in the conscience."
   C. Comes to us to liberate, comfort and reassure.

For Discussion

I. The importance of the Bible.
   A. Was Newton over-dramatic?
   B. How far has the Bible lost its unique place and power in our culture and life?

II. The Bible as a relic.
   A. Has the Bible become, for many, only a relic? List illustrations of its veneration.
   B. Consider each of the reasons suggested as to why many are turned off. Are there other reasons?

III. Rediscovering our heritage.
   A. How far should we press to get beyond simplistic answers and assertions?
   B. Should we let the Scriptures speak for themselves in progressive Revelation?
   C. How may Biblical theology and ethics guide us today?

IV. How willing are we to hear and heed the Holy Spirit?
   A. In Christian worship?
   B. In our Bible study and prayers?
   C. In time of difficult situations and decisions?

Why Pray?

Read: Matthew 6:5-18 and 1 Corinthians 14:13-15

For a very long time, indeed probably from the very beginning of their life on this planet, human beings have looked into the starry heavens and have asked the question: *"Is there anyone out there?"* You and I have asked it too, and will continue to ask. Avowed atheists, in spite of themselves ask the same question. It is likely that there is no human being who has not, or will not cry out on some occasion, "O God . . . " In this gut sense, prayer is just part of being human!

Reasons for Praying, Questions and Doubts

Why pray? There are many excellent reasons. For many of us, prayer is a channel of light and power *from* God and *to* God. We know, from experience, that when we rise from our knees we are better persons and the meaning of life is clearer. We also have reason to believe that our prayers for others help them. However, the greatest and most persistent reason for praying is that prayer is a vital and long-continuing part of *our human response to our Maker.* Before the Lord of this majestic universe, and the Lord of our own being, we bow down personally and in fellowship with other praying people in awe, wonder and adoration.

There are, indeed, excellent reasons for praying. Still, we are aware of the questions and doubts that prayer raises. We must not be afraid of these. If prayer is "for real" it must be able to stand up before even the most searching questions. Jesus taught his disciples to be unafraid of the truth. St. Paul interpreted the Christian faith in the same spirit. To the Christians in Corinth, he wrote: "I would rather speak five words with my mind, in order to instruct others, than ten thousands words in a tongue." (I Corinthians 14:19)

Many of the questions and doubts which really trouble people today concerning prayer and the Christian faith center on the alleged impossibility of believing in God, especially a personal Heavenly Father. Let us consider some of the aspects of this large and very important subject.

Some Questions and Answers

This is, indeed, a vast universe. It is far more vast, complex and mysterious than any previous age knew or could imagine. John C. Reines has expressed the sense of aloneness and futility which many feel today when he wrote: "In an age when man begins to see himself . . . as an earth-creature in a galaxy of a billion other sun systems . . . Christian realism cannot adequately provide a dike against a widening feeling of cosmic relativization, a kind of species humiliation and an ensuing sense of edgy bewilderment . . ."

Well, what about it? Is this where Christian realism comes out? How is it possible to speak of a Creator of all this — and in any way that relates to us? The impossibility of there being such a God seems to be the only logical conclusion. That is, until we consider the opposite question: How can there possibly be a cosmos like this *without* a Creator, a Supreme Mind, the Supreme Being — God — behind, in and through it all?

There is overwhelming evidence that this is, indeed, a *universe*. The word means "one song" and the evidence seems overwhelming that it is just that. However far out science reaches, there are common elements, universal equations and a majestic grandeur to be discovered everywhere. From where, then, does this supreme intelligence come? Would it not be far more reasonable to explain all the plays of Shakespeare *apart from the mind of Shakespeare* — to suggest that all his writings were formed somehow through the chance coming together of all the letters, words and sentences as the result of an explosion in a printer's shop — than it would be to try to explain this universe without reference to God?

I hold in my hand a modern watch of astonishing accuracy and observe it recording the passing minutes, days and years of earth time. I cannot believe that it came into existence by mere chance. I know for certain that behind it is human intelligence and excellent technique.

We saw on our TV screens reports that human beings conceived and produced a most sophisticated space-age laboratory and sent it out traveling at 56,599 miles per hour, directing it to explore the moons and rings of Saturn 947.6 million miles from Earth and then causing it to return pictures and much other data.

At the beginning of his *Cosmos* series, we watched astronomer Carl Sagan get into his "space ship of the mind" and sail out into the endless universe. Which is more awesome? The far reaches of space? Or the mind which explores it? Clearly the human mind is as much of a fact and mystery as is the cosmos itself. How can we account for it? No Creator? No God? No Supreme Mind to bring it into existence? Hardly!

There are, however, other questions and problems, related to prayer. There is the matter of the vast number of human beings who have lived, are now living and will live on the earth. How can even God know and care for each one individually and personally? The universal Fatherhood of God in his personal dealings with individual men and women through all the ages is mind-boggling. But it is not impossible, nor unreasonable, when attributed to the Creator of such a universe! *We must not bind God to human limitations and perspectives.*

Again, some may ask, "Why should I pray when there is no answering voice for me to hear?" It is true that God does not speak to most of us with an audible voice, but it is *not* true that he does not speak! Through the promptings and the earnest purposes which he puts into our minds and hearts, he does speak and says, Change your attitude! Overcome evil with good! Learn the truth and live by it!

God's seeming failure to answer our prayers troubles many of us. We need to accept the discipline that "No" is an answer which is quite as definite as "Yes". Those who have gone the farthest in prayer have learned to trust God whatever his answer may be. St. Paul prayed that "the thorn in his flesh" (whatever illness that may have been) be removed, but his wish and his earnest prayer were not granted, and he learned that this very refusal was the means of a wider opening of his life to God. Likewise Tagore, the famous Bengal poet, said, concerning unanswered prayer, "Thou didst save me by thy hard refusals".

Let us remember also that God cannot answer our prayer when we ask absurd things! A small boy prayed that God would make Chicago the capital of Illinois because he had written that on his examination paper. Before opening a letter, it is foolish to pray that it will not contain bad news. It is not prayer but nonsense to ask that what in fact *is* become, somehow, something other than what it is. Rather, prayer helps us to deal with the facts creatively, whatever the facts may be. *God does not save us from life's great storms and troubles but helps us in the midst of them!*

What Then Is the Essence of Prayer?

How then can prayer relate us to God, and God to us? It is most important to have a meaningful and practical understanding of this very great resource in our lives. We find the answer in the simple statement of St. Paul where he wrote to the people in the Corinthian Church, "I will pray with the spirit and I will pray with the mind also." (I Corinthians 14:13) From these few words, we may learn much for our own spiritual experience. *Let us learn that prayer is the discipline of our spirits and minds. It is the discipline which results from the voluntary subjection of our selves to the sovereignty of God in eager and sincere desire to learn and to do his will!* There are many kinds of prayer but all of them fit into and come under this truth. This is the basis for the many blessings which come through the adoration and praise of God, the confession of sin and the acceptance of his forgiveness, and our petitions, intercessions, thanksgiving and commitment.

It is not easy to pray with power and deep joy. A few mumbled words when we are tired, just before going to sleep, is not prayer at its best. Yet evening prayer may indeed be a comfort, joy and abiding blessing. At whatever time of day, we need most to give ourselves to the discerning of God's will when we are physically strong and mentally alert. Very often, we *need* to pray when we *least feel* like praying. But when we do, it may well become transforming power and joy! Praying with the spirit will go far in taking from us unkindness, impurity, self-righteousness and self-pity, and replacing them with the spirit of Christ. Praying with the mind opens vistas of truth not before imagined. We come into an awareness of how this world, in the hands of God, is a living universe. We become aware that we may love deeply, because he first loves us.

A Universal Framework of Existence

I believe that there is a universal spiritual framework of existence and that *its center is God's relationship with us and our relationship with him.* I believe that we may live and move and have our existence with a significant awareness of God in our discernment of truth and falsehood, beauty and ugliness, right and wrong, and love and hate. Day after day, these discernments may be far more than abstractions and will become utterly real in actual events and human lives. This is God's nearness to us and his presence in our lives. This is our connection with the spiritual world which is over all as well as in and through everything.

We may properly think of our awareness of God as the presence and work of the Holy Spirit. More often than not, we are not given quick and easy answers to complex questions, problems and issues. Rather we are directed to use our intelligence and integrity to work out answers, knowing that as we use the light we have, more light will come. Moreover the prompting of the Holy Spirit within our consciousness reminds us again and again of *the historic life of Jesus Christ.* He "steps out of the pages" of the New Testament and becomes our Guide, Friend, Savior, Hope and Peace.

We need disciplined times of prayer and inspiring times of worship with other Christians. Again and again we must clarify, renew and deepen our spiritual perceptions so that they do not become subjective, cloudy and self-serving. There is real danger that this may happen. But if we lead disciplined prayer lives, we will also find that many spontaneous and informal "little prayers" for guidance and strength, offered throughout the day, will not only be helpful, but will also be experiences in which he is near and very real.

FOR THE DISCUSSION GROUP

Outline

I. Our human need to pray.
   A. Our response to God.
   B. Reaching out for divine help for ourselves and others.

II. Questions and answers.
   A. How can we conceive of a "Creator" of such a vast, complex and mysterious universe?
   B. As individuals aren't we lost among the vast number of human beings?
   C. Unanswered prayer?

III. The essence of prayer.
   A. The need for a meaningful and practical understanding of prayer.
   B. Prayer, in essence, is the discipline of voluntary subjection of ourselves to God's will.

IV. The Universal Spiritual Framework.
   A. Our awareness of God in our discernment of truth and falsehood, beauty and ugliness, right and wrong, and love and hate.
   B. The witness of the Holy Spirit to the historic Christ.
   C. Personal prayer and corporate worship.

For Discussion

I. Under the starry heavens.
   A. Is there anyone out there?
   B. Without putting pressure on anyone, ask if there are those who would like to tell of occasions when spontaneously they really wanted to pray? Don't pry; respect one another's privacy.

II. If prayer is "for real"?
   A. Carefully review the questions and comments discussed in the sermon. Are they "the questions" we want to ask? What about the comments? List other responses.
   B. What other questions and comments do we want to make?

III. Spiritual discipline.
   A. How important is the discipline of oneself in meaningful prayer?
   B. Discuss the "discipline" required in the many kinds of prayer.

IV. "In him we live and move and have our being."
   A. Can God be as close to us as our own consciousness? In our thoughts, decisions and actions?
   B. How does the Holy Spirit enable Jesus Christ "to step out of the pages" of the New Testament into our lives?
   C. How may we, as praying individuals, contribute to worship? How may worship with others keep our prayer life from becoming too subjective?

The Human Being

Read: Psalm 8 and 1 Corinthians 6:9-11; 19,20

We live in a time in which it is imperative that we rethink, clarify and strengthen our Christian faith. And for this, nothing is more important — nor more difficult — than regaining a proper view of ourselves as human beings. In no other area is modern thought more confused and uncertain. The present state of bewilderment in the vital area of human self-understanding is serious for, as a person "thinketh in his heart, so is he." (Proverbs 23:7)

Confused and Inadequate Ideas

The place of the human being in the vast sweep of evolution is ill-defined. For some it seems to leave no place at all for the Creator, while for others evolution is the magnificent expression of the eternal God's creative power and continuing relationship with the cosmos, including our part in it.

We have seen the rise and decline of Freud's psychoanalysis. Today's psychiatrists are turning much more to psychopharmacology with a mixture of hope, disappointment and more than a little concern. Behaviorism, as pioneered by J. B. Watson and B. F. Skinner, has developed into the sociobiology of Edward O. Wilson which holds that the human being is only a child of nature, and completely the product of biological evolution. Morality, justice and indeed all human values have evolved only out of humankind's animal past and are secured only in the genes.

Harvard's entomologist Edward O. Wilson identifies some of the findings of sociobiology under four themes: (1) The essentially selfish basis of altruism, (2) the naturalness of male dominance and hierarchy, (3) the genetic selection of aggressivity to protect one's own resources, and (4) the instinct to protect and extend one's territory in the interest of self and nearest kin against others, especially the less able.

When human beings think of themselves in such terms and set before themselves such "values," they have moved as far as possible away from Christian teachings and concerns. Christ taught that all are God's children and that we must love and care for "the least of these." By contrast, the sociobiologists picture the successful (by whatever means) as occupying "the life boat" for survival in this world, fighting off (however brutally) those who desperately try to climb aboard. Thus the age-old struggle between love of others and caring for them; or despising them and keeping them in their place, by whatever means; is given a new name and rationale. If such thinking seems so far-out that it may simply be ignored, think again, and be more discerning of what some today are saying and doing! Anti-Semitism is again on the rise. The Ku Klux Klan is again burning its crosses and gaining in membership.

The Human Being — More Than an Animal

Let us turn now to truer and more hopeful ideas about ourselves as human beings. The concept of biological evolution may well be the best scientific view of man's relationship to the animal world. The evolvement of higher forms is beyond dispute. Moreover, evolution — in its broad sweep — has a grandeur and majesty which is truly awesome. But humans are more than creatures — we *are* creaturely — but we are also much more than that! The human being is a spiritual creature, a living soul. For this reason Christian thinkers — philosophers, psychologists and sociologists — are and must be major critics of the mechanistic and deterministic theories of sociobiology. This is being described as a "new" theory of behavior. It really is not new but a reworking of old ideas along with some laboratory experiments the significance of which falls far short of proving many of its contentions, especially as they relate to human beings and their behavior. For example, it is not proven that conflict between parents and children is biologically inevitable, nor that children are born deceitful, as it alleges. It is not proven that all human acts are ultimately selfish. It is by no means clear, certain and acceptable that all creaturely behavior, from the lowly Drosophila (fruit fly) to Homo sapiens (humankind), can be interpreted in the same way. Evolution must not be stood on its head; the most advanced forms must not be interpreted and circumscribed by the nature and limitations of creatures far back down the line.

We human beings are the result of four things: Our total biological inheritance (our genes); our total physical environment; our non-physical conditioning (what we have been taught and what we have observed); and *our personal response*. This fourth element cannot be ignored for it is most important. It is the response which we ourselves make with what we have (whether it be much or little) to all that happens along the road of life! Human beings are not puppets on strings without any real control over their thoughts, feelings, decisions and actions. Actually, to a very remarkable degree, human beings are able to change their lives, and live their lives, within their many potentialities and limitations. All of us know, or know about, some severely handicapped person who is doing remarkably well in spite of his or her difficulties. We may be such a person ourselves!

For many years, Mrs. Roblee and I have served as Fish Workers in Springfield, one day a month. Fish is a voluntary association of people who try to respond to emergency needs. One evening we had a call to go to a downtown address at five o'clock to take a handicapped person home. I pulled up in back of a special bus parked in front of the office of the State Department of Rehabilitation. Very soon handicapped people on crutches and in wheelchairs began coming out and were helped into the bus. Soon the bus was full and was about to pull away. I began to wonder why we had been called. Then, last of all, there came a severely handicapped man using two crutches and carrying a briefcase. With my help he managed to get into the right front seat of my car. As we drove along he explained that his usual driver had been taken ill and that the bus which we had seen was programmed and filled to capacity. He also said that he was the supervisor of this office! As I watched all those people and then talked with the man in charge, I realized how much people can make of themselves, and can accomplish, if they take firm control of their own lives.

Self-control is the essence of personal freedom. Indeed, this is its *definition!* We are free when we are in control of our own lives. Self-control is always a matter of degree. Some are able to control themselves better than others but, *to the degree that any* of us are self-directed, to that degree we disprove any theory of complete determinism. After watching a TV show, a small boy went around the house, walking stiffly and saying, "I am a robot! I am a robot!" Well, he is not, and God never intended for him to become one!

What It Takes to Be More Than an Animal

What does it take for a human being to become more than an animal? It takes the bringing of his or her animalistic drives and urges under control; that is, really taking charge of himself or herself. With the coming of the human being a new dimension in evolution emerged. Instead of being "pushed up" from below, human beings began to be "pulled up" from above, pulled up by means of their thinking, their hope, their faith, their goals and their love; pulled up by their spiritual capability in response to God! Lecomte de Nouy, a famous French scientist and philosopher during the first half of this century, wrote on this interpretation of evolution, but he by no means stands alone.

St. Paul, although writing in quite a different age and from a different context, parallels closely this interpretation of evolution in his teaching concerning the human being as the temple for the Holy Spirit. In 1 Corinthians 3:16 he speaks of the whole believing community as the sanctuary for God's Spirit. In the sixth chapter, he focuses it upon each individual. His teaching is that the awakened mind, spirit and body of each person should be thought of as the sanctuary for the presence of the living God.

> "Do you not know that your body is the temple of the Holy Spirit within you, which you have from God? You are not your own; you were bought with a price. So glorify God in your body." (1 Corinthians 6:19,20)

In the context of today's thought, Paul was thinking of a human being as a psychosomatic (spirit-body) person responsive and responsible to God.

It is impossible to find a greater contrast than that between this high Christian teaching, on the one hand, and sociobiology on the other. Yet this "new" behavioristic interpretation of human life is simply being accepted today by many with almost no thought, much less strong critical judgment. And it is being made the excuse for quite irresponsible life styles and the exploitation of others. In writing about sociobiology, an interpreter writing in *Time* magazine even went so far as to say:

"... the emergence of a doctrine preaching that man is caught in history, able to exercise free will only within the limits set by his genes, may do very well indeed."

(*Time*, July 25, 1977)

It may "do very well" in today's materialistic and selfish world but it will go far in causing *hell on earth!* It would be just that if each one were to do whatever caters to his desires uncontrolled by human decency, respect and concern for others, and reverence for God. The perfectibility of man has indeed fallen into disrepute because so many have tried to go it alone with no awareness of God or their need of him. We human beings must have help from beyond ourselves. We need a living relationship with God.

Cult Victims and Contemporary Society

This is not to say that all religion is good. One of the most distressing phenomena in our society is the rise of many new religious fads and cults. The People's Temple of San Francisco and Guyana became the most notorious and horrible example when some nine hundred followers committed suicide at the direction of their leader, Jim Jones. Many other cults are still flourishing and are especially attracting youth. Some make claims to Christianity, others do not. However each one declares itself to have found the "Big Answer" and demands simplistic faith on the part of its adherents. Such a fellowship has a strong attraction for those who welcome life in esoteric groups where they "belong", and where one does not have to think, but only to follow. The feeling of "security" and the joy of belonging to an inner circle of those who "know that they are right" is so great that they are willing to turn away from family, friends, associates, schools and churches. Quite literally, they welcome an "escape from freedom"!

We have said much about sociobiology and its denial of our freedom and responsibility to rise above the conditioning of our genes. Cult mentality is equally dangerous. It has been well said that, "Like sex, religion is too dangerous a subject to get wrong." Jesus was not and is not the leader of a fanatical cult. He told his first disciples, and he tells us to love and serve God with all our hearts, souls, minds and strength and to love others as we should wisely love ourselves. (See Mark 12: 29-31) God gave us *minds* to use, and we must use them. God has given us strength to endure, and we must endure many difficulties.

What Then Is Man?

What then is man? Let us make a summary of what we have been saying:

1. Endowed with freedom by their Maker, human beings are responsible for their ideas, attitudes and behavior. They are not puppets, completely conditioned by their heredity and environment. In many different ways and to varying degrees, all of us are capable of making wonderful responses.

2. It is impossible for us to overcome our evil ways, inhibitions and fears without God's help. The possibility of achieving individual maturity and a better human society rests upon the acknowledgment of our dependency upon God and our willingness to learn to do his will. In this, the historic life of Jesus is immeasurably helpful and important.

3. This does not mean that all religion is good. In fact, it may be a very terrible and dangerous thing. Simplistic teachings and authoritarian voices and cults are today symptomatic of the stressful times through which we are living. Today's young people need to be well instructed in the Christian faith and to have a viable experience of God in their homes and churches.

4. Human beings are the most dreadful and the most wonderful of God's creatures. We must decide which kind of human being we are going to be! We are capable of fellowship with God, of sharing in creation which continues, and of life beyond the grave! *This is the human being.*

FOR THE DISCUSSION GROUP

Outline

I. How do we view ourselves?
   A. Confused and inadequate ideas: Psychoanalysis, Behaviorism, and Sociobiology.
   B. The challenge to Christian teachings and values.

II. More than an animal.
   A. We human beings are the result of four things: biological inheritance, physical environment, non-physical conditioning, and personal response.
   B. The essence of freedom is self-control.
   C. "Pulled up" from above. The temple of the Holy Spirit.

III. Cult victims.
   A. "Escape from freedom."
   B. Jesus was not a "cult" leader.

IV. This is the human condition.
   A. Self-directed and responsible.
   B. Divine help needed.
   C. Not all religion is good. Simplistic teachings and authoritarian voices and cults are symptomatic of stressful times.
   D. Human beings are the most dreadful and wonderful of God's creatures.

For Discussion

I. Evolution.
   A. Is evolution incompatible with creation or a great and continuing expression of it?
   B. What is endangered by Sociobiology?

II. The development of humankind.
   A. Discuss the *four* things essential in the developing human being.
   B. Why is the fourth — *personal response* — often forgotten or not seriously taken into account?
   C. Does "freedom" have meaning apart from self-control and self-direction?
   D. Is the human being's place in evolution marked by the "pulled up" point in the development of species?

III. Cults and contemporary society.
  A. What is lacking in the education and experience of young people who join cults?
  B. Some say that Jesus was a "cult" leader. Is this true? Why or why not? What is a "cult"?

IV. What then is man?
  A. Are human beings the most dreadful and wonderful of God's creatures?
  B. How shall we live our lives? How shall we relate to others?
  C. What is the future of humanity?

The Living God

Read: Psalms 19 and 139:1-12, 17-18, 23-24
and Acts 17:22-34

We live in a time of fast moving and bewildering events, in our own country and throughout the world. We are unnerved by widespread crime and immorality, along with a bombardment of horror books and movies which exploit science and religious fiction by depicting global wars and ultimate disaster to the earth itself. We see amazing scientific and technological developments such as the exploration of Jupiter and Saturn. Fascinating color pictures of these giants among the solar planets were beamed back to earth and were seen on countless TV screens from Voyager I and II.

If it is difficult to comprehend *ourselves* (and indeed it is), it is more difficult to develop a concept of God which is believable and related to our lives. Nevertheless we must try, for the way we think about God has much to do with how we live each day. Our attitudes and actions reveal our beliefs and goals — or lack of them.

St. Paul in Athens

This was true for St. Paul and those to whom he preached in Athens. His hearers were among the intellectuals of the day who still basked in the afterglow of the greats in Greek philosophy. They engaged in much speculation, argument and discussion, but held back from making life-changing decisions. Such an audience was and is the hardest kind for a Christian teacher who wants his message really to change the way people think and live.

It is to Paul's credit that he did not shrink from such an opportunity as he had in Athens. He himself was no intellectual pygmy and his message about what God had done in Christ was not only a way of life but also the *explanation of life.* Paul's sermon that day should serve as an example for the church to follow, especially in times like these. How much we need great Christian thinkers and thinking! Across the centuries profound contributions have been made to human thought and life. There have been tragic times when the church closed its mind to new truth, and such times have seen serious dips in the witness to the living God. This must not happen now.

The record of Paul's sermon in Acts, Chapter 17, is very brief, but it does provide an outline of his thought which is remarkably helpful for us today. He began, *"Men of Athens, I perceive that in every way you are very religious."* Thus he appealed to their present perceptions and experience. If we are to win people's minds and hearts today, this is a good place to begin.

Most people, then and now, are superficially religious. They have, and relate themselves to, many superstitions and many "gods". Today the things we covet and about which we seem to care most — such as money, prestige, fine foods, cars, clothes, and the like — are not identified with shrines but are, nevertheless, *objects of worship.* In the ancient Athens of Paul's day there were many gods and many altars. Paul had just seen one inscribed to *"an unknown god."* Using this to get attention, he asked those before him to consider the living God *"who made the world and everything in it, being the Lord of heaven and earth."* How quickly he cut through their polytheism, confronting them with his Jewish monotheism (belief in the one supreme Deity). Obviously such a God is no idol made of silver or gold, nor does he live *"in shrines made by man."*

Next, Paul made reference to the Stoic belief in the unity of the human family. Paul established this unity in the work of the Creator. He said God *"made from one every nation of men to live on all the face of the earth."* Here is a profound and, in our day, an increasingly essential truth which must be learned for the survival of humankind.

Next, Paul declared that God wants us, as human beings, to *"feel after him and find him"* and that this is quite possible, for *"he is not far from each one of us."* Having affirmed God to be the Supreme Being, the Creator and Sustainer of the whole universe, he thus quickly points out that he is also immanent in us, indeed as close to us as our thoughts, feelings and decisions.

Then comes that wonderful line, *"For in him we live and move and have our being."* If this is a quotation from the philosopher Epimenides, as it is believed to be, it shows Paul's skill in reaching out to his Athenian hearers that day. A great truth is a great truth from whomever it comes!

Paul next speaks of the coming of Jesus Christ. He said, *"The times of ignorance God overlooked, but now he commands all men everywhere to repent, because he has fixed a day on which he will judge the world in righteousness by a man whom he has appointed, and of this he has given assurance to all men by raising him from the dead."* Here he points to the fact that truth and righteousness judge us. He also affirms that Jesus, sent by God, did not fail but was raised from the dead.

Did Paul himself fail in this sermon? After that address, it is reported that only a few believed and no church was established. Some commentators make much of the "failure". But consider: Luke's inclusion of this sermon among the Pauline addresses found in the Acts of the Apostles is very significant. It may well have been a bridge to the intellectual world of that time. Christian theology and the best in Greek philosophy were to have much in common. In any case, Paul used the language and some of the thought forms which were familiar to the Athenians. We must use similar skill in communication today. It is never a simple choice between "natural theology" (the God of Nature) and "revelation". Both are needed.

As we review that memorable day in Athens, let us see that the tragedy, then and now, is that mere intellectual discussions remain only such, whereas to know the truth and sustain it, life-determining decisions must be made and carried out.

The Living God

In our own times and lives, how is it possible for us to believe in a Creator-God of such a vast and complex universe? The impossibility of such a God seems to be the only reasonable conclusion — that is, until we give serious and sustained consideration to the opposing question: How can there be a universe like this *without* the Creator? Indeed, how can we account for *ourselves* — mind, heart and will — apart from such a profoundly spiritual Source? If we let these questions probe our minds and our experience, we will come up with the right answers.

Human thought never stands still and today wider vistas of

understanding are coming through a better comprehension of Process Theology. Gone is the thought of any kind of deistic Creator separated from the world and, in its place, is coming a far more profound and awesome conception of God whose presence and works are in and through the *creative process which continues eternally*. In this living universe we are not alone. Rather in this way, perhaps never before so wonderfully conceived, we do live, move and have our existence in HIM. If anthropomorphic concepts of God must be corrected, and they must be (the Creator and Sustainer of this universe is certainly not "the *man* upstairs"), even more necessary is it to reject fortuitism and aimlessness. In such a view of a dynamic cosmos, there is no place for soulless materialism.

The ancient Greeks emphasized the serenity of God, a serenity which nothing on earth or in heaven can disturb. The Stoics carried this teaching to the point of asserting that God is incapable of feeling! In complete contrast is the teaching of Jesus. Going beyond the philosophers, and even the prophetic teachers of the Old Testament, Jesus declared and showed through his own life that God does care and is very much involved in the human situation. Our Lord's ministry included the whole range of needs: physical and mental disorders, hunger and poverty, race prejudice and social injustice, women and children and every person's relationship with God.

What About Evil and Suffering?

Can we, however, really believe that God is like a good father; that he is our Heavenly Father? How can we hold onto such faith, confronted as we are by terrible evil and suffering across the ages and throughout the world? This is truly the agonizing question and the cause of the deepest doubt. At times it overwhelms us.

Such was the condition of a certain registered nurse upon whom I called one afternoon during a recent interim pastorate. As soon as she saw me she said, "You could not have come at a more opportune moment . . . How can anyone believe in God and see some of the terrible things that a nurse sees in the hospital, such as a deformed baby?" We talked at length that day, and later. It wasn't easy but gradually she found her way through doubt to faith, to an abiding faith and trust beyond comprehension.

The fact of evil and suffering is the greatest problem for any thoughtful believer in the goodness of God. However the other side of this equation must also be considered. *The fact of the existence of goodness, integrity, love and sacrifice is the overwhelming problem for the non-believer.* Without God, how can anyone account for good people . . . for Christ? Evil destroys! Goodness builds! It is on the positive and creative side of our human freedom of choice. This keeps us going, and serving, even when there are no clear answers to the horrors of life. And this is certainly true in hospital services.

Looking deeply into the eternal mysteries and seeing the revelation which God has made of himself through Christ, do we not comprehend something of what it must cost God to allow human beings to have their freedom? For this, God limited himself so that we might truly be his children. In Jesus' teaching God is not like a doting grandfather but rather a wise father who gives his children freedom of choice and then *holds them responsible* for what they decide. In no other way, as far as we can see, is character development, or the fulfillment of mature personhood, possible. Also, in no other way, can there be a close, vital and creative relationship between God and ourselves. He deals with us through the persuasion of truth and love, judgment and mercy. God allows us to sin, and to do evil to ourselves and others — and to suffer the consequences. There is a divine self-limitation in the very relationship which he has established in love, and for the profound purpose that we may truly be his human children. And, beyond all that we may think, know and do, we may completely trust his everlasting justice and mercy for all.

And God Sees That It Is Good

In the mode of the Genesis account of creation, let it be said:

1. And God looked at his vast ever expanding and very mysterious universe (mysterious, that is, to us but not to him) and said that it is good.

2. God saw our little Earth and cared about it as, indeed, he cares about every part of the cosmos, however small.

3. When the time had come, God created Adam and Eve, the Human Beings, and caused the human family to inhabit the earth.

4. God "reached down" and lifted men and women up through their intelligence and their ability to love and hope. He caused great-souled men and women, through the centuries, to proclaim that there is indeed a God — the ALMIGHTY and the ETERNAL — and to share their inspired understanding of him.

5. Beyond this, God saw the great human need for HIS INCARNATION among men and women, and JESUS CHRIST (the God-made-man and the man-made-God) became historic fact, bringing reconciliation and liberation.

6. Now God sees each one of us, and asks us to fulfill his intention for our lives by the way we think, love and live each day.

And God sees that it is good!

FOR THE DISCUSSION GROUP

Outline

I. In today's bewildering world, it is difficult to maintain a concept of God which is believable and related to our lives.

II. St. Paul in Athens.
   A. The apostle did not shrink from the opportunity he had among Greek intellectuals to interpret his concept of God. In this he shows today's Christians an approach which is needed.
   B. Paul's sermon outlined, moving from "natural theology" to "revelation."
   C. Mere intellectual discussions are not enough: life-determining decisions must be made.

III. The Living God.
   A. Pros and cons of belief: Of such a universe as science now describes how can there be a "personal" Creator? Yet, how can the universe be otherwise accounted for? From where, *from whom* did we come?
   B. The creative process continues. Anthropomorphic concepts must be corrected.
   C. Jesus taught and exhibited the compassion of God.

IV. What about evil and suffering?
   A. This is the agonizing question and cause of deepest doubt. An illustration.
   B. Yet the fact of goodness, integrity, love and sacrifice is the *overwhelming* problem for the non-believer.
   C. The cost to God of human freedom, sin and evil.

V. "And God sees that it is good."
   A. In the mode of the Genesis account of creation, we affirm our faith!

For Discussion

I. The God-concept.
   Where in the Bible can we turn for help? List some of a multitude of references.*

---

*For the development of the idea of God in the Bible, the following are a few references among a great many: Genesis 28:12-13; 32:24-30, Exodus 6:2-3; 15:3; 19:18, Isaiah 36:18-20; Deuteronomy 6:4; Jeremiah 29:12-13; Second Isaiah 43:10; 44:6; Psalm 139: 1-10; 24; Matthew 25:34-36; Mark 7:24-30; John 4:24; 2 Corinthians 4:6.

Let this show that there is long, fascinating and progressive development in the concept of deity and belief in God moving through the Old Testament and New Testament.

II. Standing Today on Mars Hill (the Areopagus — identified with the Greek Ares).
   A. List some of those today who are standing on Mars Hill, boldly and convincingly teaching ethical monotheism.
   B. Isn't the challenge now every bit as challenging as it was from Paul?
   C. Review again the outline of Paul's sermon. Is there any part of it with which we must disagree today?
   D. How may we help today's intellectuals to move from mere discussion to life-changing decisions?

III. Process theology.
   A. A lively discussion may result from consideration of the questions posed in the sermon and summarized in the Outline (see page 60, III. A.).
   B. For greater in-depth study reference should be made to studies in *Process Theology* developed out of the philosophy of A. N. Whitehead. Interpreters of this concept of God, nature and humanity include John Cobb, Charles Hartshorne, Daniel Williams, Schubert Ogden, Lewis S. Ford and Charles Birch. Dr. Birch is Challis Professor of Biology at the University of Australia in Sydney and delivered a notable paper, "Nature, God and Humanity In Ecological Perspective" at the WCC Conference on "Faith, Science and the Future" at MIT in July, 1979.

IV. The hard reality of evil and suffering.
   A Do only the secure and comfortable discuss the "problem" of evil and suffering? Must not all grapple with it from time to time, and in various ways?
   B. Can positive faith in God "keep us going" and serving even when there are no clear answers to the horrors of life?
   C. Considering the "cost" of human sin and suffering to the God of love, judgment and mercy, what must be the enormous value inherent in our human freedom and potentiality?

V. Affirmation?
   A. What now is our faith? How shall we live?

Jesus Christ
THE INCARNATION

Read: Exodus 3:-12, Luke 2:52, and John 1:1-5, 9-14

Christians believe that God, in a very fundamental way, has provided for our deepest human needs and finest achievements by giving us Jesus Christ. This he did by revealing himself uniquely in the human life of Jesus of Nazareth. This is *the Incarnation*.

It is the Christian faith that, "When the time had fully come, God sent forth his Son . . . " (Galatians 4:4) God revealed himself in nature, history and the hearts and lives of men and women. Across the centuries of Hebrew history, God showed something of his will and way through Abraham, Moses and the great prophetic teachers, but more, very much more, was to come through Jesus Christ. He was to be the very incarnation of God's own spirit, intention and love insofar as that is possible in this world. He was to be the "Word made flesh . . . the brightness of the Father's glory and the express image of his person." But how?

From the First Century to the present, those who come most completely under the influence of Jesus Christ find it necessary to say that he was both fully human and divine. This is clearly what we find in the New Testament and is affirmed in the historic teachings of the church. The concept and implications of the actual *incarnation of God* in the life of Jesus is difficult, and many do not seriously try to think it through. Nevertheless we should try to do just this for there is no study that is more deeply rewarding for our thought of God, Christ, the understanding of ourselves, and our potential as human beings. *Let us, therefore,* take with all seriousness the concept of the union of full humanity and full deity in Jesus Christ, and see where it leads us.

The Idea of Being Called

First we must consider our own relationship, as human beings, to God. One of the great messages of the Bible is that God wants each one to invest his or her time and abilities not only in a useful way but also in a particular way. Paul said, "Each has his own special gift from God, one of one kind and one of another." (1 Corinthians 7:7) Every one of us has only one life to live but our one life is incredibly rich and precious, not only to us but also to God! The amazing and wonderful truth is that the Lord breaks through the whole mass of humanity and lays his hand upon us individually and gives us our reason for being. Not all have gotten this far in comprehending Christ's teaching but when once we grasp it, and accept it, this awareness that God does have a plan for our lives greatly motivates and sustains us.

The idea of being "called" is a very Biblical concept. Over and over again, in both the Old Testament and the New Testament, we read of those who were directed by the Lord to do something, and we are told of what happened when they obeyed or disobeyed. Today, people do not like to see themselves in such an awesome situation as this and, without thinking it through, they reject its implications. Somehow they expect the professionally religious person to be "called", but they do not think of themselves in this way. However, they *should* — indeed, they *must* — if they are to understand the Bible and its message for them!

God's Intention for Him and Jesus' Response

Returning now to the consideration of God's *incarnation* of himself in Jesus of Nazareth, let us focus on God's intention — God's call to him — and his response. God wanted Moses to lead the Hebrew slaves out of Egypt and to be his great lawgiver. And Moses accepted that call. God wanted Amos to be his prophet of righteousness and social justice and, in the midst of considerable danger, this humble man did what he felt called to do. God called the "Second Isaiah" to comfort the people in their suffering in exile, and to give them faith, hope and understanding. Centuries later, when the time had come, God wanted Jesus the carpenter of Nazareth to be his true Messiah — the Lord and Savior for all men and women. Jesus' complete response to God's call and intention for his life fulfilled God's will for him and made it the great accomplishment!

Should we then think of Jesus Christ as "God-made-man" or as "man-made-God"? The answer is that both must be affirmed. It was God's intention "to send forth his Son." And it was Jesus' full response, as a human being, which made it the reality. George A. Buttrick, noted Bible scholar, said, "It is not irreverent to assume a slow clarifying of Christ's mind, a deepening awareness during his years in Nazareth that God had for him a destined and destiny-making task." In this way God incarnated himself in Jesus Christ. The New Testament record gives much information which authenticates his humanity. Luke records that "He increased in wisdom and in stature, and in favor with God and man." (Luke 2:52) We are told about his family — he had two sisters and four brothers, whose names were James, Joseph, Simon and Judas. (Matthew 13:55,56) We also are told about his occupation, his call and baptism, his praying to God, his victory over temptations, his physical needs and his joy in human fellowship. The New Testament also affirms the witness, offered by those who were with him during his ministry, that the eternal Word of God became flesh in him and we "beheld his glory, glory as of the only Son from the Father." (John 1:14)

The Incarnation Points in Two Directions

The Incarnation has great significance for us as it points in two directions — toward God and toward what it means to be fully human.

Jesus revealed what is best and possible in human nature. He showed this in his personal life-style and character. Some time ago, I made a detailed study of Jesus' character: his love, honesty, friendliness, reasonableness, firmness, intolerance, joy, kindness, holiness, etc. This has become for me not only a fascinating study but also a practical reference and challenge. Jesus made ethical and psychological considerations the pattern for his personal life and his relationship with others. And he really practiced what he preached! Without compromising his integrity he went among all types of people, enjoyed the human fellowship, loved them and sought to share with them what life may be, that is, *what God intends for it to be!* As a result, his life has been and is the foundation for countless books and sermons.

Jesus also showed what our relationship with God should be. He prayed and taught us *how* to pray. The disciples were deeply impressed with what prayer meant to him, and they asked him to teach them. Let us hear again the master Teacher on this vital subject:

> "When you pray, you must not be like the hypocrites; for they love to stand and pray in the synagogues and at the street corners, that they may be seen by men. Truly, I say to you, they have their reward. But when you pray, go into your room and shut the door and pray to your Father who is in secret; and your Father who sees in secret will reward you." (Matthew 6:5,6)

Then he gave them (and us) the Great Prayer, as a pattern.

Jesus prayed as a human being! He did not pray to himself, but to God. Nothing shows the depth of his human nature more clearly.

Jesus also revealed God, as no other ever has. This is the supreme glory of the Incarnation. He taught and made much clearer the basic spiritual nature of God. He said, "God is spirit, and those who worship him must worship in spirit and truth." (John 4:24) In his teaching, God is at once the transcendent eternal Creator and Sustainer over all the universe and also is immanent in the consciousness and life of every individual. Any reference to Jesus Christ as God on earth, of course, does not mean that God *left* Heaven or was not always the transcendent Lord over the cosmos. Rather, it means that (insofar as it is possible) Christ brought the fullest expression of the nature of God, and his intention and steadfast love for us human beings.

Through God's will and plan for his life, and his response, Jesus Christ became the Lord and Savior all of us need. As is so wonderfully stated in the Gospel of John,

> "God so loved the world that he gave his only Son, that whoever believes in him should not perish but have eternal life. For God sent the son into the world, not to condemn the world, but that the world might be saved through him." (John 3:16,17)

Jesus' whole ministry was and is directed toward enabling men and women to incarnate the spirit and intention of God in their lives. For this, however, we must see, acknowledge and reverence the great and normative INCARNATION which he was and is eternally.

FOR THE DISCUSSION GROUP

Outline

I. The nature and importance of the Incarnation.
   A. For our deepest needs.
   B. Through Jesus of Nazareth.

II. The idea of being called.
   A. Called not only to a useful life but to a *particular* life.
   B. A very Biblical concept.

III. God's intention and Jesus' response.
   A. "God-made-man" or "man-made-God"? Both Affirmed.
   B. The Incarnation points in two directions.
      1. *Our Humanity*
         What is best and possible in human nature.
         What our relationship with God should be.
      2. *His Divinity*
         Revealed God as no other ever has.
         The Lord and Savior all need.

IV. The purpose of Jesus' ministry and our response.

For Discussion

I. The idea of the Incarnation.
   A. Contrast "incarnation" with "reincarnation."
   B. Why do Christians affirm the first and reject the second?

II. A truly awesome idea.
   A. Does God break through the mass of humanity and give each of us our reason for being?
   B. What can we learn from Biblical examples?

III. Is Jesus Christ the Supreme Example?
   A. Must we believe in the full humanity of Jesus? (How else can we read the New Testament?)
   B. How far may Jesus of Nazareth be the example for all to follow?

C. What changes would take place in the lives of the world's leaders? In our own lives?
D. How far can Christ be our "inspiration" if we refuse to take him as our Example?
E. How far does our faith in him as Lord and Savior affect our answers to C and D above?

IV. How then shall we live?

What Kind of Person Was Jesus?

Read: Mark 2:13-3:6; Matthew 9:10-17; Matthew 11:2-6; and John 3:1-7,14

What kind of person was Jesus? Have you ever asked this question, and carefully considered the answer? All of us have some impression of Jesus, but how accurate and adequate is it? It is based upon what we have been taught and what we have read and heard. Too often it is supported by what we and others simply like and dislike about him. Let us be honest and admit how much we have made him according to our preferences and prejudices. We need to do better than this.

First let us remember that it is never easy to answer such a question when asked about anyone, even those whom presumably we know best. All of us change from time to time, and under varying circumstances. For this reason it is difficult even to answer the question, "What kind of person am I? We marvel about how different we are when we are with different people; each bringing out a different facet of our character. Even to ourselves we may not seem to be the "same person" today as we were yesterday or will be tomorrow. Yet we all know that somehow we are the same person through all the changes. We do have a *personal identity*.

Since it is so difficult to answer the question even concerning ourselves and those about us, why should we ask it concerning Jesus Christ? There are at least three good reasons: (1) because we have more than passing curiosity about him: something within us really wants to know; (2) because Christianity is factually based. We must know the truth! and (3) because this is a way to make Jesus more real to us!

As important as it is to ask this question about our Lord, and try to answer it honestly, we must realize that this sermon, as any presentation, can go only a short way. What kind of person was Jesus Christ? To answer this question takes *much STUDY, much REFLECTION*, and *much LIVING on our part!*

Let us suppose that in the year A.D. 30, a major newsgathering agency in Jerusalem chose one of its top investigative reporters to see and hear the Man From Nazareth who was creating such a stir in northern Palestine, and was attracting large crowds wherever he went. If there had been such an investigator, and if we had accompanied him, what would we have seen and heard, and what would he have written?

Let us now go along on this imaginary journey. Let the following be considered as from my diary.

Sunday — *Background Information*

We began our journey very early on the first day of the week. As we rested from time to time along the way, the reporter shared with us some of the background information which he had gathered in preparation for this assignment. It seems that Jesus is becoming well-known throughout Galilee. People are coming from distant places to see and hear him. The sick come hoping for a healing miracle and many have been greatly helped.

Jesus had been a carpenter in Nazareth. He was known among the followers of John the Baptist. He was baptized by John. He then went apart for a time in the wilderness where apparently he planned his ministry.

After John the Baptizer was imprisoned by Herod Antipas for having denounced the King for living in sin with his brother's wife, Jesus came preaching. Now he is boldly declaring, "The time is fulfilled, and the Kingdom of God is at hand; repent and believe in the good news of the gospel." The reporter made the observation that the Nazarene must know how dangerous such talk may be! He also told us that Jesus goes among the people as John had not. Wherever this rabbi goes, he shows compassion for the poor and sick. He teaches in the synagogues and also right out in the open. Many of his stories (or parables as they are called) are inclusive and memorable. He draws large crowds. He is praised by many, but most of the religious leaders seem unsure about him.

Wednesday Afternoon — *We Saw Jesus Himself for the First Time*

The man from Nazareth was doing unusual things for a rabbi! We would not have believed it had we not seen it for ourselves. By the lakeside, among the incoming fishermen with their catch, he went up to one of the tax collectors by the name of Levi who was sitting in the tollhouse and invited him to join his disciples, *and the publican* (the tax collector) *agreed!* That night Levi made a feast in his courtyard and invited Jesus and his disciples to come. Jesus was made the honored guest. Levi also had invited other tax collectors and their cronies to come, the very kind of people whom the Pharisees considered to be sinners because they neglect the synagogue and do not practice the laws and customs prescribed by them and their scribes. *And at the center was Jesus fellowshipping and speaking to that unholy crowd!*

The scribes and Pharisees were scandalized. Some of them looked on from just outside the courtyard and could not believe what they saw. A Pharisee did speak to one of Jesus' disciples and asked him, "Why does he eat with tax collectors and sinners?" When Jesus heard the question he said for all to hear, "Those who are well have no need of a physician, but those who are sick; I came not to call the righteous, but sinners." He likened himself to a physician — a physician of souls! And he had a startling way of interpreting it. He gave it a new twist. Indeed he spoke in irony for what he meant was that many Pharisees so boast of their goodness and righteousness that they are unaware of their need of God, and therefore are worse off than some of the irreligious who know that they need to confess and repent. This new teacher is something!

Thursday — *Feasts and Fasts, New Wine and Fresh Wineskins*

We have just had another day of surprising teachings. The Pharisees and the disciples of John the Baptizer fast twice a week, and sometimes more frequently. The people know this and many wonder why Jesus and his disciples don't fast, at least not regularly. Today some came to Jesus and asked about this. His answer was amazing! Apparently referring to something that John the Baptizer has said about him as "the bridegroom," Jesus likened himself to such a happy person and said that his joy with his disciples, and theirs with him, is like that at a wedding feast. We all know that there is no happier occasion than this. No one fasts at a wedding!

Then he said something else which is memorable: "No one sews a piece of unshrunk cloth on an old garment; if he does, the patch tears away from it, the new from the old, and a worse tear is made. And no one puts new wine into old wineskins; if he does, the wine will burst the skins, and the wine is lost, and so are the skins, but new wine is for fresh skins."

Such bold assertions shock many people, especially the scribes and Pharisees. He is quoted to have said, "Think not that I have come to abolish the law and the prophets; I have come not to abolish them but to fulfill them." Then he quotes well-known passages of Scripture and adds, "But I say unto you . . . " Each time he strikes a sharper thrust to the deeper meaning and obligation of the law concerning *killing, adultery, divorce, oaths, retaliation and hate.*

Saturday — *Sabbath Observance?*

We have just come to the end of another Sabbath. Today, Jesus and his disciples went through grainfields, and they plucked heads of grain and ate them! Some of the Pharisees, who always seem to be watching, said to him, "Look, why are they doing what is not lawful on the Sabbath?" Jesus' answer absolutely astonished them. He said, "Have you never read what King David did, when he was in need and was hungry, he and those who were with him; how he entered the house of God, when Abiathar was high priest, and ate the bread of the Presence, which is not lawful for any but the priests to eat, and also gave it to those who were with him?" Then he said to them, "The Sabbath was made for man, not man for the Sabbath!"

Later he entered a synagogue and saw a man there who had a crippled hand. Again the Pharisees were watching to see whether he would heal him on the Sabbath. Jesus said to them, "Is it lawful on the Sabbath to do good or to do harm, to save life or to kill?" They did not answer. I suppose that they could not think of anything to say. Then Jesus said to the man, "Stretch out your hand." This he did, and it was healed.

Jesus' idea that the Sabbath is made for the needs of people would appear to be a new and quite possibly a far-reaching teaching. The Pharisaic rules and regulations are primarily designed to perpetuate established customs and to restrict freedom. In contrast, are such institutions as Sabbath observance open for review and possible change? Did God really make the Sabbath for man, not man for the Sabbath? Clearly, if Jesus' teachings were applied broadly, great changes would surely take place. We might see God's intention concerning a number of things in quite a different way; we would see it focused on human values; on human welfare, happiness and liberation.

However, it is easy to see why the religious leaders would be quite unhappy over such teachings and there is a rumor that some of them have even consulted with the Herodians concerning Jesus! Yet in spite of such antagonistic feeling against him, it is said that Jesus and his disciples go regularly to synagogues on the Sabbath. They study the Scripture. They pray much to know and do God's will.

Tuesday — "Are You He Who Is to Come?"

It is now ten days since we left Jerusalem, and something happened today which could be *prophetic!* Some of the disciples of John the Baptizer came seeking Jesus, and when they found him they asked him a very searching question. It seems that the fiery John, who is now in Herod's prison, sent word by two of his disciples that he was concerned about Jesus' ministry and teaching, which is so much the same, and yet so different from his own. Speaking on behalf of John, these men asked Jesus, "Are you he who is to come, or shall we look for another?" He said, "Go and tell John what you hear and see; the blind receive their sight and the lame walk, lepers are cleansed and the deaf hear, and the dead are raised up, and the poor have good news preached to them. And blessed is he who takes no offense at me."

One who stood by and heard this reminded me that these very words are reminiscent of the passages in Isaiah which are considered messianic! John the Baptizer had spoken of Jesus as the One who should come. Is this Jesus' way of reassuring John that his hope in him is not in vain? And what words they are! What do they really mean? They warm the heart with the possibility of God's goodness coming through us to bless all people in manifold ways.

Thursday — *Homeward-bound to Report*

Well today, the reporter shared with us the account which he will file with his paper next Monday back in Jerusalem. It is a long report but I understand that the following is to be his summary statement. *It becomes incredibly personal.* I am sure that it will be given much thought by all of us as we journey.

"This assignment in Galilee has been a unique experience. I have never seen anyone like the rabbi — this Jesus of Nazareth — nor have I ever been influenced by any other as I have been by him. My life has changed . . . I mean *is changing* because of him, and by what I have seen and heard. I know that this statement does not show the dispassionate objectivity a reporter is expected to have and, indeed, what you have long found in my writings, but I cannot be faithful to the facts without revealing something of my own unexpected but profound response to Jesus!

"This man has unusual enthusiasm and joy. God is real and always seems very close to him. The very thought of God — the concept of deity — is different. God is not a theological conjecture. He is not remote but the living and present REALITY in whom we humans live and move and have our being. God is like a father to us and we are like children to him only in a way far beyond our human experience, and yet he is very much in all such person-to-person relationships.

"Jesus describes 'the gift of God' to be like 'living water' welling up from a spring in us. A still more impressive idea of his is that we may, indeed we must, be 'born again'! His exact words are, 'That which is born of flesh is flesh. And that which is born of the Spirit is spirit. Do not marvel that I said to you, "You must be born anew."

"Jesus calls God, 'My Father' and he teaches his disciples to pray, 'Our Father'. He makes much of the importance of each individual.

"Those who are with Jesus for a time, and are receptive to him, and his teachings, soon come to feel that, in a special way he shows or reveals the very presence of God. *Indeed, Jesus' supreme goal seems to be to glorify God and enjoy the warmth and power of his love.* He sees God revealed in nature (for example, in the lilies of the field), in human history and in every day life.

"He brings a new dimension to everything. There is a remarkable freshness in his way of speaking and acting. There is a whole new understanding of what religion — God — can mean to men and women, and even children. We were in a large group of people to whom he said, 'Let your light so shine before men, that they may see your good works and give glory to your Father who is in heaven.'

"You ask, what kind of person is this Jesus, this former carpenter of Nazareth? Well, I can't find just the right words to tell you, but he is very human, very down to earth, yet frankly he is different from anyone I have ever seen before. He is really filled with joy and enthusiasm for living. He is . . . wonderful!"

The above is quoted from the final report of the investigating reporter. It is amazing that he would write so, being the cool, trained and objective professional he is. Yet having accompanied him throughout this investigation, we can only agree with him. Yes, Jesus has also changed — and is changing — *us!*

FOR THE DISCUSSION GROUP

Outline

I. Why we ask the question.
   A. Deep-seated desire to know.
   B. Christianity factually based.
   C. To make Jesus more real.

II. What might we have seen and heard if we, in the company of a reporter, had journeyed to Galilee during the days of Jesus' ministry?
   A. Background information.
   B. Publicans, Sinners and Pharisees.
   C. "New Wine in Fresh Wineskins."
   D. "Sabbath made for man."
   E. "Are you he who is to come?"

III. It became an incredibly unique experience. What we learned.
   A. God is real and close.
   B. The goal of life is to glorify God and enjoy the warmth and power of his love.
   C. There is a new dimension to everything.

IV. Jesus has changed and is changing us!

For Discussion

I. Subjective and objective answers.
   A. Consider the differences between them. How may first impressions be corrected?
   B. Test them out on how we view those "we know best" and also on how well "we know ourselves."

II. We go with a reporter.
   A. Does this approach to our inquiry make it more interesting? More objective?
   B. Study the situations described in the sermon in which we "saw" Jesus. Are they the important ones?
   C. What other situations might have been chosen?
   D. Would they have significantly changed our impression of Jesus?

III. Jesus' influence on people.
  A. Who else has changed the world so greatly, and in so short a time?
  B. What did Jesus' awareness of God have to do with his power over others?
  C. What does it mean to "glorify God"?
  D. What does it mean to enjoy the warmth and power of his love?

IV. Conversion and discipleship.
  A. What does it mean to be converted? Have we outlived this idea? Do we really want to change anything in our life style?
  B. Where are we going and how well are we going there?

Confrontation at the Summit

(Palm Sunday)
Read: Mark 11 and John 16:32,33

It is obvious that God does not intend for us to live in an effortless world or in one without any dangers. Such a world, if it did exist, would not be good for us. To live, really live, we must exert ourselves. The only way anyone can run or even walk is to throw himself a little out of balance and then move his feet to restore his balance. A perfectly balanced person stands still!

We live today amid great and complex pressures and dangers. It is futile to hope that we will ever know a world without them. We must learn to live under tension and not break. Beyond this, we must learn to use the very imbalance of the world, and even the imbalance of our lives to move forward with courage and hope. We must exert ourselves.

There are many things about which we cannot "take it easy"! One of these is *telling the truth*. Another is *Christian morality*. And still another is *"obeying God rather than men."* (Acts 5:29) By its very nature, there is something fundamentally bold and immoderate about the Christian life!

In March of 1980, Archbishop Oscar Arnulfo Romero stood in the pulpit of his cathedral, and pleading with El Salvador's civilian-military junta, said: "In the name of God, in the name of this suffering people whose laments rise to the heavens each day . . . I beg you, I beseech you, I order you to stop the repressions." On Monday, while celebrating mass in the chapel of a hospital for the terminally ill, an institution which he had established, he was killed by an assassin's bullet which pierced his heart. As he lay dying he asked God to be merciful to his enemies. A few weeks before his death Bishop Romero had written to President Carter, "If you truly want to defend human rights, prohibit the giving of military aid to the Salvadoran government." To a Chicago reporter he had said, "I would be lying if I pretended I didn't care about my own life, but persecution is a sign we're on the right road. I trust in God. He is intent on having his word spread throughout El Salvador."

Necessary Boldness

Few of us want to get involved in controversial things. If we do, we are often looked upon with disapproval and said to be foolish. On the other hand, when we realize that almost all important subjects and issues are, by their very nature, controversial, we see how serious it is to refuse to get involved. Shall we settle for trivia?

What if we didn't have a free news media, a media that could not or would not uncover scandals? What if bribery, tax evasion, price manipulation and many other forms of corruption in both the public and private sectors of our corporate life were not exposed? History's shining hours have been those when men and women have stood up boldly and unperjured! There is urgent need today to meet issues squarely and with constructive boldness.

Selfishness does not work. Immediately many will say to me, "How can you say that? Look around, what else do you see?" And just as quickly, I answer, "Yes, just look around!" Selfishness simply does not work. It will not work in a marriage. It will not work in parenting. It will not work in business and the professions. It will not work in government and world affairs. Look around and see if anywhere selfishness is working out right! Oh, it may bring fame, wealth and power for a few years, but happiness, good relationships with others, and peace of mind and heart? Business people must make reasonable profits to stay in business but excessive profits and unconscionable exploitation of others, instead of solid production of vital goods and services, has brought on raging inflation and racing recession. In international relations, the will of each nation to be the most prosperous and the most secure against all others is, in this atomic age, *a suicidal syndrome.*

We criticize our government — local, state and national — and there is much that requires attention and change, but we must realize that the ways of government, on all levels, reflect accurately the way many people think and live. Changes, if they are to come and be sustained must come from close to home — that is, from us the people, including (and especially including) the Christian community! A number of years ago, E. Stanley Jones said, "We cannot live the way we have been living without having the kind of world we now have!"

It takes courage to care! Some wonderful young people in today's world have discovered this early in life. Their refusal to be indifferent or noncaring has put many parents and others to shame. Shall we, who are older, leave it to our youth to straighten things out? Surely all of us, of whatever age, owe it to God, our nation, our community, our family and ourselves to do better than that!

The Example and Courage of Jesus

When we consider all this, it helps us to understand the situation which Jesus confronted in his ministry. He came preaching repentance and the good news of the Kingdom of God. He said that the two great commandments were to love God and to love our fellows, and he joined these commandments inseparably. These are powerful and deep-searching dicta which are by no means easy to follow. It was not easy then, and it is not easy now, to obey God rather than men when all around are those who demand of us conformity and uncritical support regardless of how wrong or right they may be.

Jesus was in conflict on all sides: with the selfish, the prejudiced and the self-righteous. They hated his exposure of their ways and his demand for uncompromised integrity and concern for others. Those in places of power and influence feared the innovations he would make and how these might complicate their positions even under Roman rule. As a result they came to the point of plotting to take his life.

Jesus knew this, but vital issues were at stake, and he pressed on! This took the form of a clear-cut and very dangerous decision to go to Jerusalem with the Passover pilgrims and there proclaim the righteousness and love of God in the great Temple itself.

Jesus' entry into Jerusalem, riding on an ass, was deliberate, purposefully and carefully planned. No one knew the ancient prophecies concerning the Messiah better than did he. Some of these did not agree with his teachings concerning the Kingdom of God or his concept of his mission and ministry. Nevertheless it is clear that he felt it necessary to relate his teachings and actions to the age-old hope and expectations of his people. It was important, therefore, for him to plan carefully so that the true idea of the Messiah might be set before the people. For this he turned to the Prophet Zechariah who had said,

> "Rejoice greatly, O daughter of Zion! Shout aloud, O daughter of Jerusalem! Lo, your king comes to you; Triumphant and victorious is he, humble and riding on an ass." (Zechariah 9:9)

As Jesus rode from the Mount of Olives into Jerusalem, on that first day of a week which was to change the history of the world, the Pharisees and the Sadducees and the throng that followed him knew what he was doing — *he was proclaiming his Messiahship!*

To our modern and Western way of thinking, it seems strange that Jesus should choose to come riding on a donkey. The ass of Palestine was a fine large animal and was used in royal processions. There was an ancient tradition that when kings went forth to war, they rode upon horses, but when they went on peaceful missions they rode upon asses. The ancient Judges of Israel rode upon asses. Jesus came riding upon an ass boldly *to proclaim God's judgment and mercy.*

The next day Jesus went to the Court of the Gentiles in the Temple where the pilgrims' Roman money was discounted and changed into the "sacred" currency acceptable for the purchase of pigeons to be sacrificed. There he "overturned the tables of the money-changers" and he said to them, "Is it not written, 'My house shall be called a house of prayer for all the nations?' But you have made it a den of robbers." By his words and actions, Jesus accused the priests and the members of the Sadducean Hierarchy of desecration, commercialism in the place of prayer, dishonesty and the excluding of Gentiles. All of this was involved in "driving out the money-changers." Only a very bold man could or would have dared so to confront the Jerusalem establishment.

Why Did Jesus Do These Things?

Why did Jesus do these things? What did he hope to accomplish? These questions may best be answered by asking another. *What can be done in confronting evil?*

There are three possibilities: (1) We can *conform* to it, and even make it our goal. (2) We can *compromise* and make the best terms we can with it. Many feel justified in making this choice, and assert that no one and nothing is perfect. They don't want to be too bad, nor too good! They pray: "Dear God" and "Dear devil". (3) There is only one other alternative, and that is to meet evil with *overwhelming goodness!* Jesus chose this way.

He was one against a multitude — including all the power structure of the time, yet he dared to put *truth* against falsehood, *righteousness* against lust, and *love* against hate and selfishness. Then he trusted God for the outcome! This took extraordinary faith and courage. Jesus had both. Only hours before his death on the cross, he said to his confused and fear-stricken disciples,

> "The hour is coming, indeed it has come, when you will be scattered, every man to his home, and will leave me alone; yet I am not alone, for the Father is with me. I have said to you, that in me you may have peace. In the world you have tribulation; but be of good cheer, I have overcome the world." (John 16:32,33)

Has Jesus Overcome the World?

Has Jesus overcome the world? It is a crucial question. *The way we answer shows how well we understand him and how far we are willing to go with him in discipleship!*

Jesus' commitment and mission have had an incomparable influence on the world. Since he came the whole human experience has never been the same. There has come an awareness of goodness and, by contrast, of evil previously unknown. Although there is an ebb and flow in all historic tides, the whole course of civilization was changed, and is still being changed, by those who follow him. Nevertheless, in such a world as this, *the Christian venture* never provides such certainty that it is no longer necessary to live by faith, and we must conclude that this is the way God intends it to be!

Jesus did not live his whole life under stress, and neither should we. For many years he worked as a carpenter, taking care of his mother, brothers and sisters. He enjoyed people and had many friends. He found satisfaction in teaching, counseling and healing the sick. However, when it became necessary to go to Jerusalem in the final great venture of faith, he went. He calls us to live with hope and joy . . . *and such basic commitment,* trusting God all the way.

We need to learn how to use the imbalance of the world, and

even of our own lives, as a means of moving forward. Not many of us will die on a cross or by an assassin's bullet but all of us are called to give our lives, if need be, for God and others. Our names may never be written in any history book but God knows for what we live, and how we live, in our own time and place.

Our own high calling is to serve where we are, making the most of every opportunity. As Christ lays hold of us, we too must learn to live as he did, putting our hope and trust in God day after day.

Confronting evil with good brings victory, partly in this world and partly in the life to come. The final proof comes, and can only come, through living out our commitment. This we need to learn from Jesus Christ.

FOR THE DISCUSSION GROUP

Outline

I. We must exert ourselves amid complex pressures and dangers. Things about which we cannot "take it easy."
   A. Telling the truth.
   B. Christian morality.
   C. "Obeying God rather than men." Illustrations.
   D. Selfishness does not work. Illustrations.
   E. It takes courage to care!

II. The example and courage of Jesus.
   A. Jesus was in conflict with the selfish, the prejudiced, and the self-righteous, yet he pressed on!
   B. He came proclaiming his Messiahship and God's judgment and mercy.

III. In confronting evil, what can be done? Three choices:
   A. Conform.
   B. Compromise.
   C. Meet evil with overwhelming goodness. This Jesus chose.

IV. Has Jesus overcome the world?
   A. An incomparable influence.
   B. Yet the Christian venture must always be in faith!
   C. It can only be proven by living out our commitment.

For Discussion

I. Learning to live under pressure without breaking.
   A. Would we really want an effortless world without dangers? But where are the limits?
   B. Should Bishop Romero have taken such a strong stand?
   C. If selfishness does not work, why do so many take it for granted?
   D. In the atomic age, does international selfishness make for a suicidal syndrome?

II. Confrontation today.
   A. With whom would Jesus be in conflict today? (Be as specific as possible. Prepare a representative list. Allow for honest disagreements.)

      B. What different ideas of the Messiah are held today? Which comes closest to Jesus' teaching and example?
III. When confronting evil, which of the three choices do we usually make?
      A. How much better is it to compromise than to conform?
      B. Does choosing the maximum possible good make us strong? Does it give us greater influence on others?
IV. Living the great venture by faith.
      A. In today's world what is the relationship between "realism" and "faith"?
      B. How may we help one another?

Body and *Blood, Bread* and *Wine*

(Maundy Thursday)

Read: John 13:1-17

The Sacrament of the Lord's Supper is one of the ways Christ lays hold of many people. For numberless Christians across the years — and today — this is unquestionably true. Yet for others it is obscurantic and, even among Christians, divisive. On this Maundy Thursday, which commemorates the night when it was given, let us see what that Last Supper meant to Jesus and his disciples.

As the Disciples Remembered it

As the disciples remembered it, they were impressed by how Jesus wanted to have this time with them before he died. They recalled how he had said, "I have earnestly desired to eat this passover with you before I suffer." (Luke 22:15) They remembered how he himself had made careful plans for this meal, and how even, at that late date, they were not really aware of and, indeed, could not comprehend the possibility that their Lord would be seized and put to death. But not so Jesus! Later they came to realize that he had seen how things were going, and the awesome implications for his mission on earth which would result from Judas' betrayal and his own arrest, trial and death.

On that very night before the authorities (who were now moving with haste and desperation to end his ministry) could get to him, Jesus knew that he must "seal his teachings among his disciples" (Isaiah 8:16) as Isaiah had done long before. *This he had to do, not only with words but with a symbolism so vivid that it would never be forgotten. It would have to be done through an act that would not only involve each present disciple personally with him, but also the whole discipleship through all time!*

Who, other than Jesus, could accomplish so much in one brief hour?

Soon after they had begun to eat, Jesus rose from the supper, laid aside his garments, and girded himself with a towel. Then he poured water into a basin, began to wash the disciples' feet, and to wipe them with the towel with which he was girded. (John 13:4,5) As they had entered the room they had seen the usual pitcher of water, basin and towel. At the close of the day, it may well have been their practice to take turns washing one anothers' feet before eating. After walking over dusty roads in sandals all day it was desirable that this be done. However on this Night of all nights, inexplicably not one of them had been of a mind so to humble himself before the others by performing this task. Perhaps brought on by a growing uncertainty and fear, all of them had been in an unhappy, sour and selfish mood. Looking back to that hour, the disciples came to see that Jesus had sensed the situation and had realized that unchecked it would have thwarted all his hopes. In doing what he did, the disciples came to see how Jesus had seized the opportunity to change their feelings and whole outlook. Before Jesus had returned to his place at the table, a vision of their "Servant Lord" had come to each of the disciples.

Other incredible things happened. When Jesus announced that one of them was plotting to betray him, not one of them jumped to his feet to protect him! Instead, one after another, they asked, "Is it I?" (Mark 14:19) Had they all been so unsure of their commitment? The record speaks for itself. Before that night had ended, Judas had indeed betrayed Jesus with a kiss and, after the Master's arrest in the Garden of Gethsemane, all the others had scattered in fear and confusion. Only Peter had followed, far behind, and had gone into the courtyard of the High Priest's house where Jesus had been taken. It was there that three times over he had denied that he even knew the Galilaean. What a Passover! What a night!

Yet not Darkness, but Light

Yet, as the disciples recalled all that had happened, and had begun to comprehend it, their overwhelming feeling about their experience in the upper room was not one of darkness but of light, not of fear and despair but of hope, trust and steadfast love. For them the traditional Passover had been transformed into something new, different and transcending. It had very sharply focused the teaching and spirit of Jesus, the depth and transforming power of his love even through his death by crucifixion and, most wonderful of all, the reality and joy of his risen PRESENCE. It had become the Lord's Supper! And for those first Christians, and for us, it had become the New Covenant.

The Sacrament Today!

From the beginning, Christians have sensed the Presence of Christ in their prayers, group worship and day-after-day experiences. Unquestionably church membership and the observance of the Lord's Supper continue to help large numbers of people. For some however, skepticism and cynicism make the Christian faith and life unreal. For some, this may be especially true of Holy Communion. Instead of becoming for them the center of great truth and a wonderful means of grace, it is instead a focal point of disbelief and rejection. If this condition is to be corrected, interpretations of it must be meaningful, spiritually strengthening and, above all, honest. What, then, can the Lord's Supper mean to thoughtful and questioning people today?

Let us consider what, for many, is a point of great difficulty. In the observance of the sacraments how shall we understand "body" and "blood", "bread" and "wine"?

> "And he took bread, and when he had given thanks he broke it and gave it to them, saying, 'This is my body which is given for you. Do this in remembrance of me.' And likewise the cup after supper, saying, 'This cup which is poured out for you is the new covenant in my blood.' "
> (Luke 22: 19,20)

In that "upper room" as they ate and drank together, the disciples did not actually eat of Jesus' flesh nor drink of his blood. *In that situation, the Bread and the Wine represented his life — his total life — given for them and all others.* As he had been and was at that moment with them, so he wanted to be with them thereafter in their commemoration of him — that is, in their thoughts and feelings, in their faith and hope, and in their decisions.

If that night the bread and wine obviously had to be *symbolic* of all that he was and all that he stood for, why should these elements be considered any differently now in the celebration of Holy Communion? Far from destroying the significance of the Lord's Supper or Christ's real *spiritual presence* with his disciples, then and now, this interpretation makes them believable and very meaningful.

In the Presence of Another

Being in the presence of another person is much more than being in physical proximity to him or her. For example, in a strange city, how many times have we stood in a long line to purchase a ticket to a sports event, or stood very close to another person in a crowded subway car, and not have known those around us at all? Unless something else happened we were not in their "presence." Our knowledge of others depends upon how, and how well, they lay hold of us by sharing their thoughts and feelings, and by what they and we do! So it is with a musician in the concert hall or a pastor with his congregation. For a time at least, we may be in their "presence" because such persons are communicating with us, and we are receptive to them.

Under great stress, such as with soldiers in battle, what a comrade says or does may stay with us for the rest of our lives, especially if we have a memento that reminds us of him or the event. We "see" him again and again, and relive with him the unforgettable experience.

I believe that this helps us to comprehend what the Lord's Supper soon came to mean to Jesus' disciples. He gave to the eleven, who remained after Judas had left, not only a memory but symbols — Bread and Wine — which could periodically be set apart from their common use, for something as meaningful as HIS LIFE — who he was and is, what he stood for, and what he accomplished.

In one of many pictures of the Lord's Supper, an artist chose to picture only the Bread and Wine. At least, that is all we see at first look. Gradually, however, we become aware of the Face of Christ painted in the background. For the first disciples, the consecrated loaf and cup always helped to bring their Lord and Savior into their presence. Likewise, as we today learn about Jesus Christ from this loaf and cup, and our minds and hearts are open to his teachings and spirit, the Sacrament helps to make his Presence real to us. In this was — and is — a mingling of minds and hearts — his and theirs — and now his and ours — in life-renewing and transforming experiences.

FOR THE DISCUSSION GROUP

Outline

I. As the Disciples remembered it.
   A. They recalled how much Jesus had wanted that time with them.
   B. The washing of their feet.
   C. How they had asked, "Is it I?"
   D. Jesus' prayer and Judas' betrayal in Gethsemane.

II. Yet the Upper Room was remembered not as darkness, but light! It became focused upon:
   A. Jesus' teaching and spirit.
   B. The transforming power of his redeeming love.
   C. The reality and joy of his risen *Presence*.

III. The Sacrament today.
   A. A major help for many, but a problem for some.
   B. That night, the bread and wine had to be *symbolic*. Why should they be considered any different now?

IV. Christ's spiritual presence.
   A. What it means to be in the "presence" of another.
   B. The mingling of minds and hearts, his and ours, in life-renewing and transforming experiences.

For Discussion

I. The historic setting for the Sacrament. (A fresh study of the biblical record makes the Sacrament more meaningful and addresses some problems people have with it. Review the happenings on that memorable night.)
   A. How uncomprehending have we been on occasions?
   B. Have we been willing "to wash the feet of another" even our brother or sister?
   C. Are we ever unsure of our commitment to Christ?
   D. Do we always pray, "Not my will, but thine, be done"?

II. In the presence of Christ, what do we need to do?
   A. Confess our sins?
   B. Repent and accept divine forgiveness?
   C. Renew our covenant with Christ?
   D. Reach out in forgiveness of others?

III. How meaningful is the Sacrament to us?
   A. It is reported that in some churches attendance declines on Communion Sunday! What can be the reason for this?
   B. Do we find anything negative about it?
   C. How should we observe the Lord's Supper?

IV. May not the Lord's Supper be, or become, very important in the periodic renewal of our Christian experience and life?

He Trusted in God

(The last meditation offered in an ecumenical three hour service on Good Friday)

Read: Matthew 27:35-50 and Luke 23:32-49

How should a human being die? At first this question may be thought of as a very unwelcome question, and even quite morbid. Yet for something so universal and inevitable it should not seem to be out-of-place or even unwelcome. Moreover to have the right answer is profoundly comforting and indeed quite necessary for living now at one's best.

How should a Christian die? On this Good Friday, as we have meditated about many things, we have looked to Jesus in the supreme moments of his cross-bearing and self-giving. Now at the end, it all comes to Jesus' final witness to empowering faith.

In derision, some who saw him there on the cross in the bitterest shame and anguish, mocked him saying, "He trusted in God." (Matthew 27:43) *He did indeed*, but that was not weakness and folly but the source of profound strength and victory. This amazing fact was dimly seen by that battle-hardened Roman Centurion who stood by observing. Even in the midst of that whole gruesome situation, after Jesus died, this soldier exclaimed, "Certainly this man was innocent." (Luke 23:47) "Truly this was a son of God!" (Matthew 27:54) We cannot see these words as a complete affirmation of the Christian faith as we would make today, but it is most significant that this soldier saw Jesus, in that bitter hour, not as the weak victim of an intrigue but as the INCOMPARABLE VICTOR, in an inexplicable way, on that terrible day!

I do not understand his cry, "My God, my God why hast thou forsaken me?" as an indication that he felt abandoned by God. These are the first words of the Twenty-second Psalm, and it is much more reasonable to believe that in the unfolding affirmation of faith set forth in it, Jesus was finding comfort and sustaining strength. This Psalm contains a description of the suffering Jesus must have known. Consider the words:

"My God, my God why hast thou forsaken me? Why art thou so far from helping me, from the words or my groaning? . . .

"All who see me mock at me, they make mouths at me, they wag their heads . . .

"I am poured out like water, and all my bones are out of joint; my heart is like wax, it is melted within my breast . . .

"My tongue cleaves to my jaws; thou dost lay me in the dust of death."

BUT THEN COME THESE WORDS:

"I will tell of thy name to my brethren; in the midst of the congregation I will praise thee.

"For he has not despised or abhored the affliction of the afflicted; and he has not hid his face from him, but he has heard, when he cried to him.

"From thee comes my praise in the great congregation; my vows I will pay before those who fear him.

"Posterity shall serve him; men shall tell of the Lord to the coming generation, and proclaim his deliverance to the people yet unborn, that he has wrought it."

(Psalm 22:1, 7, 14, 15, 22, 24, 25, 30 and 31)

If his words quoted from the first line of this psalm, mean that he was recalling it (and what other conclusion is possible?) think what insight is given us both as to his terrible suffering and ignominy, and *also his unshakable trust in God!* It may well have preceded his final prayer of trust and assurance, "Father, into thy hands I commit my spirit." (Luke 23:46)

These words, too, come from the psalms. This reference is from Psalm Thirty-one, verse five which reads, "Into thy hands I commit my spirit." This is the way it reads in the ancient psalm, but Jesus added a very important word: "Father." "Father, into thy hands I commit my spirit." In the Old Testament God is referred to as the "Father" of the nation. Jesus made it very much more intimate and personal and, therefore, more profoundly sustaining.

"Father into thy hands I commit *my spirit.*" My spirit — I, my *true self, the finest, the highest and most sacred part of my being.* In living faith and trust, this means the giving of one's all to God for all the days of our years, and for the future he promises.

How does a Christian *live* and *die?* This is the way!

FOR THE DISCUSSION GROUP

Outline

I. How should a human being die?
   A. To have the right answer is of the greatest importance.

II. "He trusted in God."
   A. Although first spoken in derision, this was the source of Jesus' strength and victory.
   B. The Centurion's comment.

III. Quoting Psalm 22.
   A. Words of terrible dereliction, "My God, My God why hast thou forsaken me?"
   B. Other words of extreme mental and physical suffering.
   C. Then words of faith, purpose and assurance.

IV. The last words spoken from the cross: "Father into thy hands I commend my spirit."
   A. Jesus added the word "Father" to Psalm 31, thereby making it a very personal prayer.
   B. This is the way a Christian lives and dies!

For Discussion

I. Trusting God all the way. Which is more important:
   A. Looking back?
   B. Living in the present?
   C. Trusting God for the whole future? May any one of the three be ignored without disastrous consequences?

II. Derision.
   A. Are we, or the things we stand for, ever subjected to contemptuous or humorous mockery?
   B. In such trying and possibly dangerous circumstances what should we do?
   C. Should we reexamine ourselves and our position to be sure of the facts and our position?
   D. Then how may we keep our self-respect and personal integrity?

III. Abandoned or comforted?
   A. Some hold that Jesus was and did feel abandoned by God, and that this terrible extremity was part of the cost he paid for our Atonement — sharing the anguish of the lost in hell.
   B. Others hold that Jesus, in that terrible hour, sought and found renewed comfort in Psalm 22, and thereby *strength for serving and trusting God all the way.*
   C. Which interpretation do we believe is correct?

IV. May we too find assurance and comfort, all along the way, and at the end, in the prayer, "Father into thy hands I commend my spirit"?

Our Risen Lord (Easter)

Read: Mark 16:1-8; Matthew 28; Luke 24;
John 20 and 21; 1 Corinthians 15:1-11, 35-50

Unquestionably the greatest moment in the life of Jesus Christ, both for him and his disciples, came when God raised him from the dead. That *event*, after almost two thousand years, is of major importance in the evaluation and interpretation of Jesus and his significance for humankind.

Every Easter, multitudes bring their lives as lamps to be lighted at the flame of his triumph over death. People come to Easter services with a deep and poignant need, but not all are helped. The great blessing does not, and cannot, come with so little faith and commitment. Indeed, what can Easter mean for those who worship with the Christian community only on this day, or never come a ?

Christ's resurrection does not and cannot stand alone. That climactic development is inseparably linked to all that preceded it:

His human preparation, baptism, temptations and commitment,
The calling of his disciples,
His teaching,
His compassionate ministry,
His confrontation with those who sought power and wealth for themselves without regard for the needs or welfare of others, and consequently
His terrible suffering and death on the cross!

All this preceded his resurrection. So for us, Easter now, and every succeeding year, will mean very much, or very little, depending on how we have been thinking and what we have been doing, yes, and how we will follow Christ into our own future.

The Facts Upon Which Easter Is Based

The Resurrection of Jesus Christ is *an historical event* and this is, or at least should be, clear to all, believers and non-believers alike. It is possible to make this statement for the following reasons. The Pharisees, Sadducees and the Roman authorities all wanted to get rid of Jesus, and they had every reason to believe that they had succeeded when his lifeless body was taken down from the cross, *but they were wrong!*

Instead of lies winning out over truth, sin over goodness, and hate over love, the exact opposite became the reality.

His little band of fear-stricken disciples became a new and mighty fellowship of believers and doers.

For almost two thousand years Christ has influenced and changed history. Churches, schools, hospitals and all manner of human services have come through the influence of his teaching and compassion.

Most significantly, far greater value has been placed upon the life of each person. All ethics and morality owe him an incredible debt for far greater *reverence for life*. Even where respect for each man, woman and child is downgraded and scorned, the Christian perspective and conscience persist and remain challenging.

In view of all this, it is clear that his enemies did not get rid of Jesus, and his influence on the world came after God raised him from the dead, and was the direct result of that resurrection. Since all this may be documented, we may say, indeed, we must say that the Resurrection is an *historic event*, dated between AD 27-33 and occurring in ancient Palestine! This is the *fact* of the Resurrection.

Just *how* Jesus Christ returned to his disciples, and to humanity through them in the First Century, is a matter for careful and reverent study. The New Testament accounts do not fit easily together. There were and, therefore, still are, different interpretations. But as Walter Russell Bowie wrote in his book, *The Story of the Bible*, "through the various descriptions of the risen Jesus one great fact comes clear: the disciples who had thought that Jesus was dead knew now that he was alive; his spirit was in their midst, and their spirits caught fire from that conviction."

How, you ask? Did Jesus return in *a body of flesh and blood?* Many believe this. Others believe that the Biblical records indicate that our risen Lord was, as he is today, *the spiritual reality and presence of God.* The New Testament accounts do speak of a difference between the way he was before his death, and the way he was as he came to his disciples after his resurrection.

Still others ask, Is there *an order of existence between what we call the "physical" and the "spiritual"?* Did Christ return in some form of "spiritual-physical materialization"?

These are interesting questions, and should be carefully and reverently considered. However the essential fact is that he came, and still comes with spiritual reality and strength to those who open their lives to his love, and serve him in daring trust.

There have been a number of studies which present evidence for the empty tomb. One of the best, *The First Easter*, was completed in 1972 by Paul L. Maier, Professor of Ancient History at Western Michigan University. However, those who emphasize *the spiritual presence* also are believers in the Resurrection. After all, his *spiritual* presence is what matters, whether or not he appeared for a time in a body of flesh and blood.

In whatever way the "how" of the Resurrection is interpreted, it is clear that the disciples were not ready for what happened. At first they were disillusioned and stricken with fear. They were pathetically weak, helpless and hopeless. ("They all forsook him and fled." — Mark 14:50 "We had hoped that he was the one to redeem Israel." — Luke 24:21) How greatly they changed! They dared and kept on daring their all. They no longer feared death. The transformation was the direct result of the Resurrection, and was something which had been done for them, not something which they accomplished by and for themselves.

In summary, therefore, it must be said that the Resurrection was a quite specific event in the history of the world when Jesus Christ returned to his first disciples with reality and transforming power.

What His Resurrection Means to Us

What did Jesus' Resurrection mean to the world? What does it mean now, for us? Death was, and for many today continues to be, the most disturbing fact about our human existence. If death ends all, what sense does this world make? What about injustice and human suffering? If this is all, how could God, if he is like Jesus, have made a world like this? What about *reverence for life* itself? If, at last, all comes to naught, why care about anything? Deep within the human consciousness, the wish to survive is far more than selfish egotism; it is deeply and inevitably part of our cry for some true meaning and purpose in living. If we believe that there is nothing more, life *now* becomes increasingly bitter.

This was true in the ancient world and, despite our modern sophistication, it is just as true today. Our modern suppression of the fact of death, as much as possible and for as long as possible, is a *copout*, a refusal to face one of the obvious inevitables. It is not an indication of good mental health but the opposite; it is an unresolved obsession with the whole subject.

One of the greatest contributions which Christianity made when it emerged in the ancient world was at the point of its *transformation of the meaning of death*, and Christ's Resurrection was the powerful event that brought about the change. There is nothing today which our distraught world needs more than for the disciples of Jesus to recover invincible trust in God now and forever more; and to astonish the world with the good news in Jesus words: "I am the resurrection and the life . . ." (John 11:25)

He Came . . . He Comes!

Two thousand years ago Jesus Christ came to his disciples huddled in fear behind locked and barred doors. Later he was seen by more than five hundred people at one time. He came to Mary Magdalene, whose life was transformed. He came to Peter, who had denied him three times. He came to many others, including the two disciples as they journeyed to Emmaus. We read that, "While they were talking and discussing together, Jesus himself drew near and went with them." At first they did not recognize him (which is not surprising). Had Jesus not died? Does a dead man walk along a road? He questioned them. He opened their understanding to what he had taught them about the Scripture. And then, at the dinner table, "He took bread and blessed it, and gave it to them. And their eyes were opened and they recognized him." (Luke 24:13-35) What a picture of the risen Lord with his disciples!

And *now* he comes to each one of us, individually, if we will have it so. How beautifully and powerfully Albert Schweitzer expressed it for all who are morally in earnest and spiritually awake:

"He comes to us . . . as of old, by the lakeside, he came to those men who knew him not. He speaks to us the same word: 'Follow thou me!' And sets us to the tasks which he has to fulfill for our time. He commands! And to those who obey him, whether they be wise or simple, he will reveal himself in the toils, in the conflicts, the sufferings which they pass through in his fellowship, and, as an ineffable mystery, they shall learn in their own experience."

In any carefully considered perspective, EASTER commemorates the greatest event in all history! How greatly also we should regard Christ in our own personal experience, and in our faith and hope.

At first, Jesus' crucifixion seemed to evidence once again that the life and work of a good and helpful person had come to a dismal, horrible and heartbreaking end. But now that terrible day of sin and death has become *Good Friday*. The *Cross*, that instrument of torture and death has become the greatest symbol of faith and dedicated service. And *Jesus* himself has become the *Christ-of-God*, the *Ruler* over life and death! (Romans 5:21)

This, for all time, is the meaning of his *Resurrection*, and our *Easter!*

FOR THE DISCUSSION GROUP

Outline

I. Christ's Resurrection cannot stand apart from his life.
   A. Not all are helped at Easter services. It depends upon how we have been thinking, what we have been doing, and how we purpose to follow him into our own future.

II. An historic event.
   A. His enemies did not succeed.
   B. His incomparable influence.
   C. The fact of the Resurrection may be dated and located.

III. How Christ returned to his disciples.
   A. A matter for careful and reverent study. Different interpretations:
      1. A body of flesh and blood.
      2. The spiritual reality and presence of God.
      3. In some way between the "physical" and "spiritual."
   B. In any case, the disciples were surprised and greatly changed.

IV. Its meaning for us today.
   A. Transforms death.
   B. He comes to us.
   C. The overcoming of evil with good.

For Discussion

I. The observance of Easter.
   A. Contrast secular ways of observing Easter with the Christian celebration of Christ's Resurrection.
   B. How should we as individuals and families observe the day and the week?

II. The Christian faith is historically established.
   A. Discuss the difference between fiction and historic fact.
   B. Discuss the beginning of the Christian era (Anno Domini) with other First Century historic developments.
   C. What difference does it make if the life of Christ is historic?
   D. Why must we put the evidence for his life in literary and historic perspective?

III. Distinguishing between the "fact" and the "how" of the Resurrection.
   A. Why is the "fact" more certain than the "how"?
   B. Review carefully all the Biblical references to the Resurrection. Let this indicate why reverent and honest interpretations differ.
   C. Should such study detract in any way from the joy of "'knowing" our Risen Lord?

IV. Christian living is living in faith.
   A. What difference does it make *now* if we really believe in and trust God for life and fulfillment beyond the grave?

The Meaning Of The Cross For Us
Read: Mark 10: 35-45

Over the last several weeks we have been reminded of some of the great moments in the teaching, ministry, death and resurrection of Jesus Christ. Now, on this first Sunday after Easter, and in the light of the divine Revelation that came to humankind through him, let us look more intently at the meaning of the cross — for us and the world.

In every Christian church, the cross is the central symbol yet its meaning, *as defined by Jesus himself*, both in his teaching and in his life, is not well-understood, and even less well-practiced. Jesus said, "If any one would come after me, let him deny himself and take up his cross and follow me." (Matthew 10:38) What does this mean? At the very least, it means some deep soul-searching, and some significant life-changing!

The Way of the Cross

The way of the cross is the highest road of Christian outreach, love and service, and it is exacting.

When we suffer involuntarily some severe loss or affliction we often say that this is our cross to bear, but this is to misunderstand the cross in its truest meaning. To be sure we must bear, with good faith and strong courage, inescapable sorrow and tragedy, and for such difficult times we are assured of God's comfort and help.

In contrast to this, however, the way of the cross means the anguish, danger and suffering we experience when *voluntarily* we stand for something or do something which, *although not imposed or inescapable,* is nevertheless in line with our Christian love and duty. It is something we do quite apart from any benefit which may come to us. Indeed it is something we do because it is right to do it even though it is, or may be, to our own disadvantage and even peril.

This understanding of the cross is clearly to be seen in the teaching, suffering and death of Jesus. It is also to be seen in the lives of his first disciples. When St. Paul bravely endured the physical ailment which he referred to as his "thorn in the flesh" (2 Corinthians 12:7), he witnessed to the divine grace which was given to him to bear the suffering and to rise above it, but this was not "bearing his cross"! However, he and Silas (his missionary companion) were following Christ in the way of the cross when they showed compassion for a demented slave girl, and deprived her owners of the money they were making out of her affliction and, as a result, were beaten and thrown into prison.

What it means for us now to live by the principle of the cross changes day after day. So do the issues which we confront. I have never seen a crucifixion and I never *want* to witness any such horror unless, in some way, I might be able to help the victim. This is the normal reaction of sane and healthy-minded people. But today, some people nurture a perverse desire to see violence and even blood-letting depicted on the screen or in a TV show, and will attend a sporting event with even greater interest if there is to be some blood while, at the same time, they avert their eyes and close their minds and hearts to the very real suffering of others all about them! As followers of Christ, we need to get such attitudes reversed. Giving himself for the redemption and salvation of others, giving himself for the reconciliation of men and women to God and to one another, Jesus endured the shame and agony of the cross.

It was said of a certain minister that "for tender souls, he served up half a Christ." This we must not do. Being the one he is, Jesus Christ must be interpreted honestly and with historic accuracy. So also must be our discipleship. Only then can we be faithful to the lived-word of God, our Lord!

Jesus' death on the cross is the supreme example of redemptive sacrifice, but the way of vicarious love runs all through life. Many years ago a medical doctor went to China as a missionary. The area where he was serving became plague-infected. People all about were dying. He made a culture of the disease and took some of it to America in the hope of finding a cure. It did not work out as he had hoped. The making of an antitoxin was difficult and costly, and in his homeland there was not enough concern felt for a solution. With a heavy heart he returned to China. There he found still more people suffering and dying. A point came where he could no longer endure his own ineffectiveness in the terrible situation. He went to his laboratory and swallowed some of the toxin and then took the first ship to America. His destination was a famous medical center in Baltimore. On the long journey he kept an accurate record of his case. By the time he reached the hospital he was in a coma, but all knew his plea that whether or not he recovered, there should be unceasing effort until an antitoxin was developed and made available. In order to save others, he could not save himself!

The most vital approach to an understanding of Jesus is not through any theological statement, however true, but by way of an attitude toward life, an attitude of commitment to God and to others. Jesus gave his all to God, and to others. He did not hold back even though the cost of living that way led to his crucifixion. As a result, he is the one in all history who touches our lives most vitally, and lays hold of us by the mysterious and incredible love and power of God.

On Ash Wednesday, February 16, 1983, the Reverend John Worcester, a Presbyterian pastor in Anaconda, Montana, in an act of planned civil disobedience, illegally entered the protected area of a nuclear missile site. Protesting the U.S. and Soviet arms race, he was arrested and jailed in Great Falls, Montana. Prior to his protest, he asked his congregation for a six-month leave of absence, without pay, to "stand boldly in absolute opposition to the billions of dollars spent for nuclear arms . . . while tens of thousands of children die each day because their simple, basic needs go unmet." In support of his action, his church granted him a leave of absence with housing and pension allowance. Whether we agree or not with his way of personally protesting *the insanity of the nuclear arms race*, we cannot fail to see in his action a contemporary illustration of taking the way of the cross in love and concern for others, and to back up one's personal conviction with costly action.

It is unconscionable that Jesus' death has been used across the centuries by some misguided "Christians" as justification for persecuting and killing Jews. Calling them "Christ-killers," these sadists and murderers have planned and participated in horrible persecutions. Such violent hatred led to the pogroms in Russia and Poland in the late Nineteenth Century and to the Holocaust, the systematic destruction of over six million European Jews by the Nazis before and during the Second World War. And now, as incredible as it may seem, such irrational and diabolical hatred is again on the increase in Europe and even in the United States. True Christian believers are and must be heartsick over expressions of prejudice, hatred or violence against those of the Hebrew faith and culture. It is impossible to account for the death of Jesus without making reference to the part played by the religious leaders at that time but this does not, and must not be allowed to place a stigma on all the Jews then or since. *Nothing could be more of a repudiation of Jesus' own attitude, mission and ministry!*

Theological Interpretations

Let us now turn to theological reflections on the cross. An event having such profound meaning and consequences as the crucifixion of Jesus Christ was, and still is, interpreted in different and somewhat inconsistent ways. A discerning reader of the New Testament comes to realize that there is not just one but different interpretations of the death of Jesus. *All of them relate to the tragic estrangement between human beings and God, and the divine measure taken through Christ to bring about reconciliation and salvation.* Beyond this there are two main lines of interpretation.

One of these interprets Jesus' death on the cross in the tradition of *the Jewish sacrificial system.* This is quite understandable in view of the first disciples' familiarity with that system. In their need to find words with which to comprehend and share what had happened, inevitably they made use of the idea of sacrifice. The shedding of Christ's blood in the crucifixion seemed to fit into the ancient pattern, and bring it to fulfillment. The writer of the Letter to the Hebrews put it this way:

> "He entered once for all into the Holy Place, taking not the blood of goats and calves but his own blood, thus securing an eternal redemption. For if the sprinkling of defiled persons with the blood of goats and bulls and with the ashes of a heifer sanctifies for the purification of the flesh, how much more shall the blood of Christ, who through the eternal Spirit offered himself without blemish to God, purify your conscience from dead works to serve the living God." (Hebrews 9: 12-14)

Thus the author of the Letter to the Hebrews saw Jesus himself as the great high priest who leads us to an awareness of our sin and makes us aware of the divine grace which opens to us a new righteousness, a new hope and a new life! These and other similar passages in the New Testament have a rich symbolism, the meaning of which becomes comprehensible through the study of the Old Testament. But superficially interpreted they have led to shocking misrepresentations and unethical perversions of the Gospel such as the idea of Christ's death as a *ransom* paid to God or the devil for the release of sinners. Years ago, Arthur John Gossip, theologian at the University of Glasgow, correctly identified such thinking as a "hideous heresy, and the blasphemy of blasphemies."

The other New Testament interpretation of the cross is more understandable and applicable for us today. In it the cross shows and emphasizes Jesus' commitment to truth, righteousness, justice and love — and his own great faith and trust in God. It shows him as the greatest teacher and exemplar in the tradition of the Old Testament prophets. And this interpretation is clearly emphasized in Jesus' own teachings.

As far as it is recorded, Jesus used the word "ransom" on only one occasion. In that situation he was concerned to emphasize how different his followers should be from those who "lord it over" others. The tenth chapter of the Gospel of Mark records how James and John, among Jesus' first disciples, came asking him to give them preferential treatment. We are told that Jesus called his disciples to him and said to them:

> "You know that those who are supposed to rule over the Gentiles lord it over them, and their great men exercise authority over them. But it shall not be so among you; but whoever would be great among you must be your servant, and whoever would be first among you must be slave of all. For the Son of Man also came not to be served but to serve, and to give his life as a ransom for many." (Mark 10: 42-45)

Let us try to feel the impact of this teaching as it must have come to his quarreling and preference-seeking disciples, and as it should come to us.

In interpreting God's will for his life and theirs, Jesus said, *"For the Son of Man came not to be served but to serve, and to give his life as a ransom for many."* (The word "ransom" has several meanings, including "redeem" and "set free." In the context in which Jesus uses the word here, what Jesus teaches is the power which comes, through those who accept the servant role, to transform, redeem and set free those who are bound by their own selfish and unloving attitudes. This is for their salvation. To be part of this *ransom* may be very costly. For Jesus, and some of his disciples, it meant going the full way of the cross. It is because God so greatly loves us that he gave humankind the life, teaching, death and resurrection of Jesus Christ! But to have this redemption, we must make our own response. Just as God-in-Christ lays hold of us, so we, by faith and love, must lay hold of him.

For Jesus this was God's way of reconciling human beings to himself, and of effecting their reconciliation with one another. For us the great joy and wonder in the Christian faith and life is that Christ has provided for reconciliation on both levels.

So What Does It Come To?

A bishop of the Roman Catholic Church tells this story. In Paris, many years ago, three university students were walking down the street. It was Good Friday and they observed people going to church to make their confession. As is the case today with many young people, these students were most critical. On an impulse, they challenged one of their number to go into the church and tell the priest what they thought.

So, on a dare, one of the young men went into the church, and came into the confessional and said to the priest, "Father, I have come merely to tell you that Christianity is dying and that religion is a superstition." The priest received this statement calmly and replied, "My son, why have you come here to tell me this?" The student then told of his two friends, and of how he had entered the church on a dare. The priest said, "You accepted one dare tonight. Now accept another. Go to the front of the church. Look up into the face of Jesus there on the cross. Then say, 'Jesus died for me and I don't care.' Say it again. Say it a third time."

The young man felt foolish, but he accepted the priest's dare. He made his way up to the front of the church, knelt and looked up into the face of Jesus. Slowly he said, "Jesus died for me, and I don't care." Then more slowly and hesitantly he repeated the words. He began to say a third time, "Jesus died for me, and . . ." but was unable to finish. Getting up from his knees, he made his way back to the priest. "Father", he said, "I am now ready to make my confession." The bishop concluded his account with the statement, "I know that this story is true — I was that young man!"

As we see Jesus there on the cross, can we say, "He died for me and I don't care"? Is this our answer? Or, from the depths of our hearts do we say something quite different? *I do care! Truly this man was and is the Son of God! And when he asks me to go beyond self-interest, when he asks me to take up my cross and follow him, I can and will do it! God will be my helper!*

FOR THE DISCUSSION GROUP

Outline

I. The meaning of the Cross, as defined by Jesus himself, is not well understood, and even less well-practiced.

II. The way of the Cross. Jesus said, "If any one would come after me, let him deny himself and take up his cross and follow me."
   A. The way of the cross must be differentiated from *involuntary* suffering.
   B. Strictly speaking, it means standing for something or doing something which, *although not imposed or inescapable*, is in line with Christian love and duty.
   C. The above distinction between the two types of suffering is seen in Jesus' teaching, suffering and death, and also in the lives of his first disciples. An illustration.

III. Following in the way of the Cross.
   A. Jesus must be interpreted with historical accuracy and heroic action. Illustrations.
   B. Attitude is more important than creed.
   C. Anti-Semitism condemned.

IV. Theological interpretations.
   A. Different interpretations in the New Testament:
      1. In the tradition of the Jewish sacrificial system.
      2. In the tradition of the Old Testament prophets.
   B. The latter is emphasized in Jesus' own teaching. (His use of the word "ransom")

V. "Jesus died for me . . . and I *do* care!" An illustration.

For Discussion

I. The central symbol.
   The Cross is and must continue to be the central symbol of Christianity, but is there urgent need to go back to its origin and redefine its meaning?

II. The cost of discipleship.
   A. How many people seriously consider Jesus' awesome invitation to take up the cross and follow him?

B. Is "the way of the cross" defined by distinguishing between *involuntary* suffering, and suffering and danger incurred *voluntarily* for the sake of Christian love and duty expressed toward others? Give contemporary illustrations.

III. Who then can or will follow?
 A. For our own sake and other "tender souls" should we not settle for "half a Christ"?
 B. Does our *attitude* bring us closer to him than any creed can?
 C. Why is Jesus' own attitude, mission and ministry a complete repudiation of anti-Semitism? (See Luke 23:34)
 D. Why do Jews and Christians especially need one another today? (The Judeo-Christian tradition is threatened.)

IV. Cheap grace.
 A. Do some interpretations of the Atonement lend themselves to "cheap grace"?
 B. What is wrong with this? How dangerous? How may it be avoided or corrected?

V. At the foot of the Cross.
 A. What effect does it have on us to kneel before Jesus Christ, who died for us, that we might follow him in faith, and in service to God and other human beings?

For Christ's Sake

Read: Paul's Letter to Philemon

In this letter we have for our consideration one of the most inspiring stories to come out of the New Testament church.

The word *sake* is a strong and moving word. Out of deep love and respect for someone or some cause, we say "For the sake of . . ." When we do something in a particular way we may use the word, as for example, "For the sake of clarity, I will speak slowly." When we make an appeal to others to help someone, some group or cause we say "For the sake of . . ." When we make reference to the Ultimate Standard or Principle, we say (if we are thoughtful, and not swearing), "For God's sake . . ."

In Paul's letter to Philemon, as it is translated in *Today's English Version*, this word "sake" is used five times. Some critics may complain that this is too much repetition of the same word in a few sentences. From a literary point of view, such criticism may be justified but repetition does *underscore* the key thought which Paul wanted to convey to his friend and fellow Christian, Philemon.

He reminds him that all the members of the Christian community are motivated and held together by their love for Christ and their obedience to his teaching. In essence, he is saying, *we are what we are for Christ's sake!*

Paul's Letter to Philemon

One of the shortest books in the Bible, only one chapter in length, is Paul's letter to Philemon, yet for many reasons, it is also one of the most interesting and important writings in the whole New Testament. It comes from a very dramatic moment in Paul's life and ministry. At the time of its composition he was a prisoner, probably in Ephesus. Some time before this, he had been instrumental in the conversion of Philemon who lived in Colossae. It was then that he had become acquainted with one of Philemon's slaves, a man by the name of Onesimus. In those days, Greek slaves were often very well-educated men and even from rich and cultured backgrounds. As provinces continued to fall to the Romans, the number of such slaves increased. It is quite possible that Onesimus was one of these. He had stolen from his master and had run away. Now there was a price on his head! We are not given any details, but somehow Onesimus got to Ephesus where he met Paul again, and was led to accept Christ.

Both Paul and Onesimus were then confronted with the problem of his relationship to Philemon. Should he continue to be a fugitive? Should he stay in Ephesus where perhaps he could be a helper to Paul and other Christians? Should he return to Philemon where, under the laws and customs of the times, his master had the right even to put him to death?

The decision was that regardless of the consequences he should return to Philemon and that he should carry a letter from Paul. That, to say the least, took daring faith and considerable courage. Let us review what Paul wrote in this letter:

> "I make a request to you on behalf of Onesimus, who is my son in Christ; for while in prison, I became his spiritual father...
>
> "I am sending him back to you now, and with him goes my heart. I would like to keep him here with me, while I am in prison for the gospel's sake, so that he could help me in your place. However, I do not want to force you to help me; rather, I would like for you to do it of your own free will...
>
> "It may be that Onesimus was away from you for a short time so that you might have him back for all time...
>
> "How much he means to me! And how much he will mean to you... as a brother in the Lord... Do this for the Lord's sake!"

This obviously is a very personal letter yet it also refers to the Church which met in Philemon's home. Apphia and Archippus are also mentioned by name as members of that congregation. It was written in the faith and with the clear expectation of a miracle of Grace. What happened? The very fact that it was saved for future generations to read is highly significant.

Paul's faith in the power of Christ in the life of Onesimus, in the life of Philemon and in that Christian group which met in his house was justified. Quite apparently all were transformed. His letter was not a frontal attack on the institution of slavery but a powerful appeal to the mind of Christ and for something to be done out of loyalty to him — something done *for Christ's sake* — and it was, as George Buttrick has written, the "seed that finally split the rock of slavery."

Across the years and today — *for Christ's sake* — has been and is a powerful Christian motivation.

Not for Christ's Sake

Not all those among the followers of Jesus, even in the New Testament, learning the meaning of living for his sake. Even among the Twelve there was one who would not really learn of Jesus and be steadfastly committed to HIM. His name was Judas! He wanted Jesus to fulfill his own selfish desires and goals, and when our Lord showed that he had quite a different orientation to God and men, he betrayed him and helped to bring about his crucifixion.

There is no record that Judas did anything to help anyone. We, however, must assume that he had good potential for discipleship otherwise Jesus would not have chosen him to be among the Apostles, but he spurned that call. He denied his Lord and, after betraying him, took his own life. He experienced no miracle of Grace, no power of the Holy Spirit. He wrote no part of the New Testament. He contributed only to the selfishness, cynicism and despair in the human experience.

His tragic life has always held a strong fascination for many people who realistically see themselves mirrored in the confusion, frustration and final disillusionment of Judas. This, in addition to the new style of music, is the reason for the attraction which the Rock Opera, *Jesus Christ Superstar*, has had for so many people, especially young people in this disenchanted age. Because it has to do with Jesus and the very center of our Christian faith, we need to look at it carefully and thoroughly.

Tim Rice and Andrew Webber, who produced *Superstar*, state, "Basically, the idea of our whole opera is to have Christ seen through the eyes of Judas." When this is done, there is a very dramatic effect. To see the story of Jesus from the point of view of Judas is to see it *upside-down*. What this leads to is clearly suggested in the libretto.

These words give an incredible and fantastically wrong picture of Jesus. For example, he is depicted as one so distraught that he needs to be soothed and comforted by the presumed prostitute Mary Magdalene. In "The Last Supper" scene, he is made to say,

> "I must be mad thinking I'll be remembered — yes I must be out of my head!"

and after his betrayal of Jesus, Judas in self-pity exclaims,

> "Christ, I know that you can't hear me
> But I only did what you wanted me to
>
> "God! I'll never ever know why you chose me for your crime
> For your foul bloody crime
> You have murdered me! You have murdered me!"

Yes, it makes quite a difference when we try to see the story of Jesus from the point of view of Judas because we see it upside-down.

In order to see the life, teaching, death and resurrection of Jesus rightside-up — and find our way out of the nightmares of Judas — we must see Jesus through the eyes, hearts and lives of Peter and Andrew, James and John, Paul and Barnabas, Mark and Luke and all the rest who found, in Jesus Christ, the miracle of God's Grace, the transforming power of the Holy Spirit.

Miracles Wrought by God's Grace

As we have seen in Paul's letter to Philemon, those first Christians expected miracles of Grace to take place in their relationships within the Christian community — and they were not disappointed. Today, we need to make much more of the church and not write it off in seeking solutions to individual problems and great social issues. Paul could call upon Philemon to honor his Christian commitments because he had learned what it meant to live and work for Christ's sake.

Why has the church, in our day, been so downgraded by many people? The reason is that very often the church is no better than other organizations. Let's face it: without the influence of Christ, the church is no better than any other human organization. Indeed, it is quite a bit worse. This is true because its implicit expectations go unfulfilled! What many of its critics, both in the church and outside of it, are saying is, "I had a right to expect more, much more of the church, but this is what I find: jealousy, selfishness, unkindness and the whole gamut of human cussedness." And they can make a case for their criticism. But what such people don't understand or quite possibly don't really *want* to understand is that they are a part of the problem; indeed, perhaps even more a part of the problem than others, as long as they only stand aside and criticize! We need to have faith in the miracles of Grace in and through the church, *when it really is the Church, with Christ in the central place.*

What happened in the relationship between Philemon and Onesimus was indeed a miracle of Grace. Paul asked Philemon not only to forgive and free his slave but also to encourage him in the Lord's work. In the letter itself the position of Onesimus is not made explicit but it is clear that Paul wanted this new convert to be welcomed and made active in the Christian community. There is evidence that precisely this *did* take place and that, after a time, this former runaway slave became the great early-church Bishop Onesimus of Ephesus!

Further, some scholars believe that he may have been the one who brought together the most important letters of Paul for inclusion in the New Testament. *In support of this likelihood is the inclusion of this very letter.* If Bishop Onesimus did gather Paul's letters so that they might be preserved and circulated, is it any wonder that he included this one which Paul had given him to carry to Philemon; this one which is so brief and *so different* from all the rest; and this one which saved his life and gave him his ministry in the First Century Church!

There is much, therefore, that all who have come after him, including ourselves today, owe to the miracle of Grace which took place in the mind and heart of Onesimus, Philemon, and that little congregation which met in his home.

So now, in these times, *for Christ's sake*, we must carry on the true mission and ministry of the Church.

FOR THE DISCUSSION GROUP

Outline

I. A personal letter.
   A. It is a letter written by Paul, but including Timothy, to Philemon and the church that meets in his house.

II. The background.
   A. Paul had been instrumental in the conversion of Philemon and the formation of the church in Colossae. There he had met Onesimus, a slave of Philemon. This man had stolen from his master and fled. Somehow he met Paul, who now was in prison in Ephesus, and was converted.

III. The problem at issue.
   A. Should Onesimus continue a fugitive, stay in Ephesus and help Paul, or return to Philemon?
   B. The decision was that he should return to Philemon, bearing this letter.
   C. There he might receive harsh treatment, even death or, as Paul pleads, he might be forgiven and welcomed as a brother in Christ.

IV. For Christ's sake.
   A. The powerful motivation of the church in the First Century.
   B. But not all were faithful -- *Judas!*
   C. To see the story of Jesus from the point of view of Judas is to see it upside-down as portrayed in *Jesus Christ Superstar*.

V. Miracles wrought by God's grace.
   A. In the life of Philemon and the church. The preservation of this short letter indicates a wonderful story.
   B. Did Onesimus become the Bishop of Ephesus?
   C. Did he gather Paul's letters for inclusion in the New Testament?

For Discussion

I. For Christ's sake.
   A. Consider the word "sake." Although the Greek word

"dia" occurs only once (in the ninth verse) the TEV translators have caught the point and power of Paul's entreaty when they use "sake" five times. In essence Paul is saying, "As Christians, we are what we are for Christ's sake."

II. Today's church.
   A. Try to think of Pauline-type ministries today. Are there any?
   B. In spite of greater difficulties, the church in the First Century seems to have been more virile than the church today. Why?
   C. What may we learn from the church in the First Century?

III. What is the responsibility of the Christian community toward:
   A. Prisoners in penitentiaries which don't even try to be effective *correctional* institutions?
   B. Refugees from war, poverty, hunger and hopelessness?
   C. The physically and mentally handicapped?
   D. The segregated poor among all races and cultures?

IV. Upside-down.
   A. Why do so many delight in trying to turn Christianity upside-down?
   B. Does its inherent validity and strength make it the target for abuse?
   C. Can Christians approve of *Superstar?*

V. Expectations.
   A. Paul had great expectations through his faith in Christ and his love for Philemon and the others in the Christian community in Colossae.
   B. What about our faith and expectations? How may they be strengthened?

Loving and Being Loved

(Mother's Day)

Read: 1 John 4:7-21

"What makes for happiness?" In one way or another, all of us ask and try to answer this question. The answer that often comes to mind has to do with material things, power and prestige. No one can deny that such considerations have a place in our happiness. Yet to make them all-important, or even central, is like trying to hold dry sand in our bare hands. The more tightly we close our hands upon it, the less we have!

Upon what, then, does happiness depend? Happiness and unhappiness are the by-products of many things, especially personal feelings and relationships. In the early days of "Breadbasket" (later "Operation Push"), Jessie Jackson, the civil rights leader in Chicago, could be heard over the radio directing his large Saturday morning audience in the repetition of "I am somebody." It was an important step toward greater self-respect for many. The happiness of any person depends upon making the most of one's abilities and opportunities and thereby being respected by others.

There is another and still deeper and truer answer to being happy. On its highest level, it depends upon *loving and being loved!* Every person is born with the ability to love, but if this ability is never awakened or is sharply restricted, or perverted, then deep and true happiness is impossible. Everyone has the need to love and to be loved. God knows this, and answers our need. It is a great affirmation of our faith that God answers our need for love by opening his heart to us. He awakens our love, and deepens it by loving us.

The writer of the First Letter of John puts it very clearly. "We love because he first loved us." (1 John 4:19) In this way we are taught the reciprocity of love. We cannot receive love's blessing unless and until we give love in return. *This is the most important lesson we human beings have to learn.* It is true for single people, married couples, young people and senior citizens. It is true for all of us.

On a Monday evening, as we drove home from a conference, we listened for two hours to a radio program from Chicago. It was all about the large and growing number of single people in our society. Four persons participated: three had been married and divorced, two had children, and one had never been married. All were "successful." Two were professionals. Perhaps the most notable thing about the whole discussion was that they seemed to be agreed that marriage was a very high risk, and that it was failing in today's society *and should be avoided!* They spoke about many aspects of the marriage-failure syndrome, but always with reference to one's personal gain or loss, to what one was getting or not getting out of it. Not once did they see that the real trouble is today's "me-ism" or self-centeredness. Not once did they see marriage providing the basis for the highest human happiness through loving another person deeply with honor and respect, and being so loved in return.

Love Between Husbands and Wives

We don't have to do anything to have an unhappy home; but we have to do a great deal to have a genuinely happy one. For the husband it means, "I love her and she loves me." And for the wife it means, "I love him and he loves me." What is so necessary, and so wonderful, is a face to face, heart to heart, and life to life kind of love.

Here is a code for married happiness that does not come from any one marriage or from any one author; rather it has in it the wisdom of many couples and a "heap of living" together.

1. *Never let romance wane.* The benediction at the marriage ceremony doesn't end romance. It only provides a faithful man and woman the opportunity to be permanently romantic, and on a level unimaginable to the promiscuous.
2. *Never let both husband and wife stay angry* for very

long at the same time. Let one partner, at least, be calm and rational enough to keep the perspective.
3. *Never shout at one another*, unless the house is on fire!
4. *Never find fault* unless it is perfectly certain that a fault has been committed. Even then, always speak lovingly.
5. *Never part for a day* without loving words to remember during absence.
6. *Never meet without a loving welcome.*
7. If at all possible, *never let the sun go down upon any anger* or grievance.
8. *Recall frequently the happy hours* of early love and romance.
9. *Never sigh over what might have been*, but make the most of what is.

I am convinced that there is no marriage, the deep joy of which could not be enhanced by the periodic review of such a list and the renewed commitment to practice more faithfully what is known to be the way of mutual respect and courtesy.

I am quite aware that such a code of married happiness will seem to some hopelessly old-fashioned, and that at certain points it is different from the ideas and practices of some consultants who make much — overmuch, I think — of liberated sex, of being frank and honest and giving full expression to one's feelings, personal desires and expectations. Frankly, I am not impressed with much of this "new wisdom." Some of these counselors are themselves divorced, and unhappy and maladjusted persons. Perhaps they could learn something from the many couples whose marriages are stable and deeply rewarding to the partners themselves and to others who know them. Let us make love authentic and strong right in our own homes so that there is no need and little desire to try to find it in someone else's home.

There is something still deeper and more fundamental. The love of a husband for his wife and the love of a wife for her husband needs a still greater love. Always, in all human relationships, and not least in marriage, we need to be very much aware of the love and purpose of God and of our love, commitment and joy in service to others which we give in return. The only one whom we should love more than our husband or wife is God. Our love for God never detracts from our love for another person; it raises it to the highest point. The Seventeenth

Century English poet, Richard Lovelace, expressed the truth clearly in one of the lines of a poem, "*I could not love thee, dear, so much, loved I not honor more.*" The highest, finest and most enduring love between husband and wife is not achieved by two people gazing fondly at one another but by these two partners in life looking out from the same vantage point and venturing boldly together to fulfill God's purpose for their union, and their individual careers or roles both within and beyond their home.

Parenting

Love's reciprocity is also important between parents and growing children. Every child needs to learn the meaning and reality of love from his or her parents. *The child learns to love because he or she is loved.* On a recent afternoon, I stopped at a street corner where school children were crossing. I observed a little girl running happily across the street to her mother who, instead of a loving embrace, slapped her child across the face. I don't know why that woman acted so (perhaps she had had a hard day) but as the now tearful little daughter tagged along after her, I felt sick to my stomach. What a disgrace to parenthood! What trouble she was making for the future!

One of the most deeply disturbing problems in today's society is the increasing incidence of battered children and incest. Why do parents mistreat their own little ones? Studies show that parents who do such horrible things were themselves abused by their parents. One would think that such people would be the first to care lovingly for their children. But no, it does not work out that way. Why? The answer is really not hard to find. Their parents did not love them so they never learned to love. Their lives were never touched by true and deep caring. In spite of this, the cycle can be broken.

What does it mean for parents to love their children?

It means to love them *before they are born;* indeed, even before they are conceived. They must be planned for and really wanted. We must also plan for their physical, moral and spiritual well-being after they are here.

It also means *love without possessiveness.* We beget our children but we do not possess them. This means that we must love them with unqualified love. We must accept them because they are our children, regardless of whether they please or displease us. Only as we acknowledge them as our own can they properly accept themselves. Such self-identity and self-acceptance is quite essential to their growth and achievement.

(In passing, let it be noted that this is the same great truth which we Christians see in God's acceptance of us!)

There is a *great venture of faith* which parents make in each one of their children. No one can know in advance the outcome of another person's life — and that includes the lives of their own children. Nor is it the responsibility entirely of the parents, for society and especially the young person has much to do with the way things go. Wise, therefore, are those parents who, simultaneously, subordinate their wishes to the free choice and decisions of their children, but who also try, by word and example, to surround the whole family with the greater love and purpose of God for each one of its members.

It means taking *the birthright* of their children very seriously. In a home where this is done, love's reciprocity becomes much more probable. Growing children learn to love because they first are deeply and wisely loved. Here, therefore, is the question for all parents: If you were choosing someone whom you had to trust to educate your children, to teach them to be honest and good citizens, to lead them to live morally clean and physically healthy lives, and to bring them to Christ and significant participation in the church, *would you — could you — conscientiously choose yourself?* Some parents, perhaps unconsciously, expect more of the public school teacher, the boy- or girl-scout leader and the minister and church school teacher than they do of themselves. They have no right to do this. And their hopes have little foundation if they do, for they themselves are among their children's most influential teachers.

Parents Without Partners

Many of those whose marriages have not worked out and are divorcees with children, feel that the church has turned its back on them and is less than helpful. Insofar as this may be true, it is one of the most serious indictments that can be made against the contemporary church, and one of the greatest challenges to change and demonstrate Christ's love. A divorce may be the best alternative in view of unresolvable problems. And when, for better or worse, it has taken place, life must go on and the need for loving and being loved is greater than ever. This need of deeply distressed people presents a challenge to every congregation. All about are lonely people and confused and troubled children.

In addition to divorced parents there is a growing number of singles (men as well as women) who have never married but who adopt a child and do an excellent job of rearing a boy or girl who otherwise would be an orphan. Such surrogate parents are to be commended and encouraged, and they and their children need relationships with other families. Providing for this should be another, and a very important, aspect of the church's outreach and ministry.

Amid all the complexities and problems of today's society, one thing is certain and paramount: *the importance of the family.* It is central to the happiness and well-being of all. Once, all of us were children and had — or failed to have — a good home. On this Mother's Day, let us rejoice in the Christian family heritage, and make the most of reciprocal human love. *We must love because God loves us!*

FOR THE DISCUSSION GROUP

Outline

I. What makes for happiness?
   A. Four things suggested: Material possessions; power and prestige; self-respect; and loving and being loved.
   B. The destructive power of selfishness. An illustration.

II. Love between husbands and wives.
   A. A code for married happiness.
   B. Some of the "new Wisdom" questioned.
   C. The only one we should love more is God!

III. Parenting.
   A. How the child learns to love.
   B. Why do some parents mistreat their children?
   C. Parental love means:
      1. To love them before they are conceived.
      2. To love without possessiveness.
      3. To encourage freedom and show love by word and example.
   D. The birthright of every child.

IV. Parents without partners.
   A. A major responsibility for the church.
   B. Surrogate parents.
   C. The importance of the family.

For Discussion

I. The pursuit of happiness.
   A. Why isn't it more successful?
   B. Do we have to pursue something else in order that happiness may be its by-product?
   C. Is the highest happiness the by-product of reciprocal love?

II. For married happiness.
   A. Discuss the "code." What should be changed or omitted? What should be added?
   B. Should we put our love for God above all other loves? What does this mean? How may it strengthen human love?

III. Learning to love.
   A. Let each one think back over the years and answer the question, How did I learn the meaning of love? And the companion question: Have I learned it well enough to share it with others, especially my own children?
   B. Let the group work on a comprehensive written *birthright*, listing items which should be accorded every child.

IV. One-parent families.
   A. How well is our church doing in providing a place for and helping such families?
   B. How may it be improved?

Men, Women and God
Read: Mark 10:2-16; John 4:4-43; John 14:6

Men, women and God — these are the participants in the greatest drama of all, the human experience; and each has a role to play in it.

Invited to Live

More than any other teacher who has ever appeared on this earth, Jesus has invited and inspired men and women to live — live at their highest and best. It is a vital affirmation of the Christian faith that he came forth from our Creator with a special message about how to live as we are intended to live. If we were to buy a fine automobile, with all the latest improvements on it, and fail to learn how to drive it as it should be driven (if, for example, we drove it only in low gear and with our foot constantly on the brake), people who knew us would say, "How foolish! How absurd!" Soon we would have a very poor opinion of ourselves. Such misuse or abuse of a fine car is as nothing, however, in comparison with the way some people treat their own bodies, minds and souls through promiscuous sex, too much food, chain smoking, alcohol and other drugs, and the like.

Misuse of one's self — body, mind or spirit — is indefensible from any worthy point of view, and becomes extremely reprehensible when it also involves another actual or potential human being. Family planning to bring wanted children to parents who are ready and able to take care of them is a very high expression of Christian stewardship. On the other hand, abortion — in cases where the mother's life is not seriously threatened — to limit the number of children a woman may have, or to reduce excessive population — is the least defensible way of trying to handle an unwanted pregnancy. In defense of abortion it is urged that a woman should have the right to choose. Of course she should! She should always have *the choice not to become pregnant!*

It is incredible that in our society today, many teenage girls are having babies or abortions! One shudders to think of what this means for these child-mothers and the little ones they bring into the world. There can be no good future for a society whose members allow such conditions to continue. It is argued that a fetus is not a human being until considerably more development has taken place, but no one can deny that it is a *potential person*, not some lower form of life. To regard it otherwise is to undermine the sacredness of human life, responsibility and privilege. It can never be enough to teach young people the physiology of sex without clear and strong references to morals, that is, the importance of their own clean living, respect for those of the opposite sex, and, most of all, the birthright which should be provided every baby. Such elementary morality should be assumed and taught, as it was for a long time, in our schools. The presumption should be that no boys or girls should become "sexually active" until they are old enough to understand what they are doing. They need to understand how they may become too seriously involved with one another and quite possibly with an unexpected child.

A group of young unwed mothers and the Catholic Archdiocese of Denver are now helping teenage couples to set dating limits. They are advertising and making available buttons which may be worn on dresses or coats with NO inscribed on them. The message is understood and effective. Many young people are welcoming this way of making their feelings clear before and during any date.

Beyond such elementary morality, the church has a great responsibility and opportunity to lift up, before both youth and adults, the nature and joy of the Christian family experience.

In Today's Adult World

Now let us look at the adult world. About eighty percent of American families include both a father and mother. Does this mean that, as a way of life, the basic family pattern is secure? It is perhaps better than some, in pessimistic moments, may have imagined, but it is hardly good. Since 1970 the divorce rate has risen 100 percent, bringing the number of divorces close to nine million men and women. Many of these are trying to carry on as single-parent families. In view of the situations out of which many have come, including those involving battered spouses and children, divorce may be the essential first step toward a better future. Rarely, however, is the situation without serious difficulties for the adults and the child or children. It is not easy to be the breadwinner, the homemaker, the loving parent when wise parenting is most needed, and to adjust oneself to an adult career and social aspirations. Sometimes things get far out of line. A single-parent father came home late one night and heard the sound of a girl's voice coming from his son's bedroom. The next morning the son asked his father if he minded that his girl friend had spent the night. Before his father could answer, the son said that he shouldn't mind since he (the father) often brought his ladylove home. In another home a seven-year-old son asked his mother's visiting business friend if he planned to spend the night. And there is another mother who reported that she required her dates to leave in the early morning before her young daughters got up.

All of us in the adult world would do well to take a clear and fresh look at Jesus' teaching and see its relevance for today. There is reason to believe that Jesus would find a great deal of which to approve and support in the women's liberation movement which is spreading around the world. Against the background of long-established traditions which made the position of women in the family and in other areas of life subordinate to men, his position was radically different and very much more liberal. At the same time he lifted up principles of justice and righteousness so strict that they went beyond the prevailing patterns of morality then, and still do today. When we look closely, we discover much in the teaching of Jesus and in his actions which show his very positive attitude toward women who, although with some different and very important roles to play in life, are *coequals* with men.

In the Sermon on the Mount, Jesus said, "You have heard that it was said, 'You shall not commit adultery.' But I say to you that every one who looks at a woman lustfully has already committed adultery with her in his heart." (Matthew 5:27-28) It is amazing how often the most significant part of this teaching is missed. At once we see the reference to the licentious passions of men (and women) and the going beyond and behind the overt act of adultery to its erotic antecedents, but too often we miss the main thrust, namely the looking upon a woman (or a man) not as a person but as a chattel, a thing to be used to satisfy sensual and fleeting pleasures. Lust is the opposite of high regard and deeply caring love and is the root of the iniquities and degrading attitudes with which women have had to contend across the centuries. Jesus never tolerated the degrading of women or men. He would completely condemn the "Playboy" attitude; women are not "bunnies" nor sex objects.

Nowhere is Jesus' compassion for women seen more clearly than in his denunciation of the divorce procedure of that day. His approach was not to lower marriage standards but to raise them to the heights. In order to understand the position he took, we first must see the injustice then prevailing. Under Mosaic Law and in the patriarchal family pattern which still continued at the time of Jesus' ministry, wives lived under the domination of their husbands and had an uncertain future. If a man wanted to be rid of his wife, all he had to do was to write out for her a "bill of divorce" which left her in a desperate situation. Apparently some of the Pharisees heard Jesus speak against this system which allowed for such insecurity, injustice and cruelty so they came "testing" him. They asked, "Is it lawful for a man to divorce his wife?" He answered them, 'What did Moses command you?' They said, 'Moses allowed a man to write a certificate of divorce, and put her away.' Jesus said to them, 'For your hardness of heart he wrote you this commandment. But from the beginning of creation, God made them male and female. For this reason a man shall leave his father and mother, be joined to his wife, and the two shall become one . . . What therefore God has joined together, let not man put asunder.'" (Mark 10:2-9)

This well-known passage needs careful interpretation. First, we should see that Jesus spoke with discernment when he said that "for the hardness of your hearts" Moses had commanded that a certificate of divorce be given. As harsh as it was, it was better that some legal status, rather than nothing at all, be given the rejected wife. Having made this point and shown the root of the injustice, he then lifted up the whole matter to its highest level, namely, God's intention for husbands and wives in the creation. This teaching must be considered in the context of the circumstances under which it was given and must be seen also in light of *the compassion and understanding he showed divorced women.*

In this connection his visit with the Samaritan woman at Jacob's Well in Sychar is very significant. Let us lift out those parts of the narrative which especially indicate his attitude toward one who had been humiliated and divorced by five husbands. It is unlikely that any other Jewish teacher of the day would have spoken with a woman in a public place. The fact that she was also a Samaritan adds to the unusual nature of the conversation, and underscores *Jesus' acceptance of her as a person*. To her he gave some of his most important and inspiring teachings. "Whoever drinks of the water that I shall give him will never thirst: the water that I shall give him will become a spring of water welling up to eternal life." (John 4:14) "The hour is coming, and now is, when the true worshipers will worship the Father in spirit and truth, for such the Father seeks to worship him. God is spirit and those who worship him must worship in spirit and in truth." (John 4:23-24) He asked her to go and call her husband and heard her say, "I have no husband." (John 4:17) The fact that five husbands had divorced her and that she was not married to the man with whom she now lived did not keep Jesus from seeking her best good, and helping her to reach out to others. He sent her into Sychar and we read that "Many Samaritans from that city believed in him because of the woman's testimony, 'He told me all that I ever did.'" (John 4:39) The Samaritans came and invited him to stay with them, and he stayed for two days. "And many more believed because of his word." (John 4:41) Truly, this is an illuminating incident showing Jesus' understanding, compassion and constructive attitude toward women in that male-dominated society. And Jesus' teaching and attitude have importance for us today.

The Christian Family Experience

It was only an hour before the marriage. The rehearsal for an elaborate wedding had taken place the night before. The prenuptial dinner had been a very happy affair with many toasts for the bride and groom. At high noon the whole wedding party and the pastor had come together for the taking of pictures before the ceremony which was to be at two o'clock. It was about one o'clock and I was standing by a window in the south aisle of the sanctuary when the best man came over to me. After a few moments of perfunctory conversation he said with unexpected seriousness, "Can marriage today really work?" I said, "Yes, I am sure it can. Why do you ask?" He replied, "Well, sir, I wonder. My girl and I were planning our wedding but now it is all off . . . there are so many questions . . . and I see so many unhappy couples . . . so many failures . . . things are so different . . . today marriages aren't working out very well."

That conversation stays in my memory as an illustration of the contradictions and predicaments many of our finest young people feel in these times. I suggested that marriage is not failing but that *many of today's presuppositions* are proving to be seriously wrong. They are: "Pre-marital sex is not only desirable but even advantageous for marriage" . . . "Sex, within marriage, is the central thing" . . . "What I can get out of marriage is more important than what I can contribute and share with my partner" . . . "If it doesn't work, I can get a divorce" . . . "Marriage is for the convenience of two career-minded adults and it is not necessary to give much thought or planning as to how husband and wife may complement one another instead of moving toward separation" . . . "Let us never have a family; children will only make things difficult." Such thinking can only add up to trouble, quite probably big trouble.

On the other hand Christian marriage can and will work out wonderfully today if husbands and wives make the right preparations and deeply love one another within the framework of God's love and plan for them. The rules are neither "old" or "new" but are in the very nature of the human experience in this high and holy relationship. "From the beginning of creation, God made them male and female . . . and the two shall become one." *Whom therefore God brings together in marriage let not them, nor anyone, weaken or destroy it.*

Men, women, and God! — all this, and much more needs to be said. And in it all, Jesus' teaching is of central importance.

FOR THE DISCUSSION GROUP

Outline

I. How to live and how not to live.
   A. The importance of Jesus' life and teaching.
   B. Misuse of body, mind or spirit indefensible.
   C. Family planning, a high expression of Christian stewardship, but abortion undermines the sacredness of life, responsibility and privilege.
   D. All young people need to be taught elementary morality.
   E. Family life despoiled.

II. Jesus' teaching and example.
   A. Liberation plus strict justice and righteousness.
   B. Lust interpreted and condemned.
   C. Against the background of harsh divorce laws, he showed compassion and redemptive skill.
   The Samaritan Woman

III. The Christian family experience.
   A. "Can marriage today really work?"
   B. Many of today's presuppositions are seriously wrong.
   C. Christian marriage still can and will work out wonderfully.

For Discussion

I. God's intention in Jesus.
   A. Discuss the revelation Christians find in the life and teaching of Jesus (Galatians 4:4; 2 Corinthians 4:6; Matthew 5-7; John 1:12-14 and 13:13-17; etc).
   B. What other categories of self-abuse might be listed? Try to list all of them according to their seriousness. Are the "less serious" to be condoned?
   C. Do all forms of promiscuous sex undermine the sacredness of life, responsibility and privilege?
   D. Who and what hold back a return to the teaching of basic morality in all our schools? Should there be a wider use of "No" buttons?
   E. What about parents who say one thing and practice another?

II. The Women's Liberation Movement.
   A. How important is ERA? What would be accomplished? Are there real dangers? (If so, try to state them factually.)
   B. How would Jesus' teaching and example advance, retard or change the liberation movement?

III. The Christian family.
   Since there will be an ever increasing number of employed wives, how can husbands and wives plan better:
   A. To complement one another in their careers? How may serious conflicts be resolved?
   B. To provide essential prenatal care for the expected son or daughter?
   C. To give their child or children good parenting?
   D. To provide for their "male" and "female" roles in the family, church and community. *These and related questions challenge the future!*

The Holy Spirit and the Day of Pentecost

Read: Acts 2

If we are to understand the meaning of the Day of Pentecost and its significance for us, we should begin with the doctrine of the Trinity: God, the Father; God, the Son; and God, the Holy Spirit. Christians are monotheists; we believe in *one* God. Yet the concept of the Trinity is important and, when understood, is very helpful.

Christians Are Trinitarians

God, the Father, helps us to think of the living God — the Supreme Being, the Eternal, the Creator and Sustainer of the whole universe. At first, it may seem absolutely incredible to think of the Supreme Being as our Heavenly Father. Yet just this is both intellectually possible and quite necessary if we are to have any adequate thought of God. How can we account for *ourselves* if the Source of our life is not at least as personal as we are? Obviously God is infinitely beyond us in every way, but surely not less in any way. God is transcendent over all and yet he is very much in, through and — in every way — very much part of our day to day life.

This brings us to the concept and doctrine of the Holy Spirit. As the familiar and beloved hymn expresses it, "He has the Whole World in His Hand." As spiritual reality, God is everywhere in the world. This means that God is not only over all, but very close to each of us. Day after day as we think, plan and pray, God is as close to us as our thoughts and decisions. In our very consciousness we may be aware of him, and of our life in him.

Perhaps it may help if we think of God's presence everywhere as we think of the radio and TV electromagnetic waves which are all about us. We are not aware of them at all unless and until we tune in with them. There is, however, a profound and wonderful difference between these radio and TV communications and the presence of God. A radio or TV show is just that — a show with many listeners and viewers, but something very impersonal. When however, we pray and open our minds and hearts to God, the Holy Spirit in us becomes a very personal experience. To change the figure of speech, it is like having a very private and personal conversation with a loved one or dear friend. He knows our name. He knows all about us — indeed, far better than we know ourselves. Our awareness of God and our communication with him may become, *after a time of much praying and responsible living*, a very "one-to-one" relationship. God is there in our deepest thoughts, feelings, decisions and actions.

There is also a third and very important aspect of the triune God, and this is God, the Son, which is the reference to the historic Jesus Christ. Actually, through Christ we human beings have come to God the Father and God the Holy Spirit far more clearly and wonderfully. This becomes possible because in Christ God incarnated himself in an actual human being. Jesus of Nazareth lived and taught on earth, gave himself in vicarious love, died on a cross, and was then raised from the dead. He was truly and deeply human, and he is God's supreme way of showing us how we, as human beings, should live. He was a man, but more than a man. This was the only adequate way those who witnessed his historic life could express their experience, and their faith. They declared, "You are the Christ, the Son of the living God." (Matthew 16:16) And when we now open our minds, hearts and lives to him today, this also becomes our witness and deep conviction.

During his ministry, it was evident that Jesus had a vivid awareness of the presence of God. His disciples sensed this and through him also felt God's nearness. Jesus told them that this awareness of God would continue with them and that the Holy Spirit would point to him and would help them to understand and apply his teachings. His words were, "I have yet many things to say to you, but you cannot bear them now. When the Spirit of truth comes, he will guide you into all the truth . . . He will glorify me, for he will take what is mine and declare it to you." (John 16:12-14) Jesus also said, "You will receive power when the Holy Spirit has come upon you; and you shall be my witnesses in Jerusalem and in all Judea and Samaria and to the end of the earth." (Acts 1:8) God gave us the historic Christ for our better perception of himself, and for the guidance of our own lives.

Pentecost

We are now in a position to comprehend what happened on the Day of Pentecost. It does not and cannot stand alone but becomes meaningful and believable when we remember Jesus' teaching, ministry, death and resurrection as a whole. He promised his disciples that they would receive power when God's spirit would come over them and inspire them. After the initial amazement and joy of the Resurrection, they felt certain that there was more to come. They remained prayerfully expectant. Increasingly they were open and ready.

On the Jewish calendar, there were three festivals which, in that first century, every male Jew who lived within twenty miles of Jerusalem was legally required to attend. Many came from greater distances. These festivals were the Feast of the Passover, the Feast of Weeks or Pentecost, and the Feast of Tabernacles. For Jews, the Feast of the Passover commemorated God's freeing of the Hebrew slaves from bondage in Egypt. However for the disciples of Jesus, in addition to this, the Passover had suddenly become vastly more meaningful. *It was associated indelibly with Jesus' death and resurrection.*

The Feast of Weeks or Pentecost, on the Jewish calendar, came just fifty days later and celebrates the gathering in of the first fruits of the harvest. Possibly more people would have been in Jerusalem for this than even the Passover. As noted, the disciples were expecting more wonders to come, as Jesus had promised, and they may have wondered if the celebration of Pentecost might be the occasion.

Next, for the gaining of an understanding of what occurred let us take note of the sermon which Peter preached that day, especially his quotation from the writings of the Prophet Joel, with reference to "The Day of the Lord." (Acts 2:17-21 and Joel 2:28-32) The many references in both the Old Testament and the New Testament to this "Day" are important for an understanding of both Hebrew and then Christian interpretations. For the Hebrews there were two ages — "The Present Age" and "The

Age to Come." The latter was to be the Golden Age of God's Glory and of Israel's. However, between the two, there was to come the "Day of the Lord." They saw this as the Day of Judgment of the world and the terrible birth pangs of the new age, as vividly described by Joel. For Peter and the Apostles, after the Resurrection, the "Day of the Lord" had indeed come to Israel and the world through the life of Christ! This is what Peter declares in his sermon. What he and the others did not know was just when it would become clearly and powerfully manifest. Perhaps they had wondered, could it happen at the time of the Feast of Weeks or Pentecost? They waited expectantly.

Then it happened! The Holy Spirit came over them in a very special way, and thereafter, they were Spirit-led people. They became men and women possessed of amazing courage and power. From that day to this, such great spiritual happenings can't entirely be described in words. To what does the mention of "tongues as of fire" (Acts 2:3) actually refer? Not all will agree with any single interpretation. Yet it seems certain that it is best thought of in some symbolic sense. No one was consumed, nor even burned; but what a vivid and moving way to describe their feelings! Did not Moses hear God's call to him from a "burning bush"? (Exodus 3:2-4) The "burning heart" became the central symbol for John Calvin and, recalling his own conversion, John Wesley spoke of his heart being "strangely warmed." What does the reference to each one hearing "in his own native language" (Acts 2:8) mean? William Barclay, the well-known professor of New Testament at the University of Glasgow in Scotland, reminded us that there was no need for several languages to have been spoken since all would know Aramaic Hebrew or Koine Greek, which at that time was the universal language. He suggested that what was happening was that each person, with amazement, heard in his own mind, heart and soul God's truth for him or her!

The Significance for Us

Is the Pentecost experience only something that occurred a long time ago? Has it any meaning for us today? *The first Pentecost brought the empowerment of the disciples for the proclamation of the divine message given to the world through the life, teaching, death, resurrection and ascension of Jesus Christ. This marked the beginning of the empowerment of the mission of the church across the ages.* It was something God did for the first disciples and those to whom they witnessed. The Holy Spirit transformed Peter and the apostles. They were no longer weak and vacillating but persons with conviction and influence. Among them the Christian Church became alive and enduring. It is something that God, as the Holy Spirit, has done over and over, and will do again today.

When Peter and the apostles were confronted by the religious and civil authorities and commanded not to preach about Christ, they were able to declare, "We must obey God rather than men." (Acts 5: 29) Centuries later when Martin Luther was told to renounce his ninety-five theses or be excommunicated, he was enabled to answer, "I can and will retract nothing . . . Here I stand; I can do no otherwise: God help me! Amen." And when, while Adolf Hitler ruled as the seemingly invincible dictator in Germany, Pastor Martin Niemoller was ordered to swear allegiance to him or go to a concentration camp, this Lutheran churchman was enabled to say, "I will not acknowledge that anyone occupies a place above that of Jesus Christ. God is my Fuhrer!"

The measure of what the Holy Spirit may mean to anyone depends upon the kind of person he or she is becoming or is willing to become. Likewise, the measure of what the Holy Spirit may accomplish in, through and with any congregation depends upon the kind of congregation that church is becoming. This is what Peter declared when he said, "We are witnesses to these things, and so it is the Holy Spirit whom God has given to those who obey him." (Acts 5:32) On that first Pentecost, Peter told the people about Jesus Christ and called all to repentance and mission. In this he spoke of God's judgment and mercy. If the Apostle were to stand before us today, would he not proclaim the same message?

The Pentecostal call also has a very personal meaning for each of us. In his letter to the Galatians, Paul contrasts the "works of the flesh" with the "fruit of the Spirit." "Now the works of the flesh are plain: Immorality, impurity, licentiousness, idolatry, sorcery, enmity, strife, jealousy, anger, selfishness, dissension, party spirit, envy, drunkenness, carousing, and the like." (Galatians 5:19-21) In complete contrast is his reporting of the work of the Holy Spirit: "The fruit of the Spirit is love, joy, peace, patience, kindness, goodness, faithfulness, gentleness, and self-control." (Galatians 5:22-23)

Our life is meant to be lived from a center, a divine center, within each of us. The reality of the Holy Spirit may be known as we keep this, the sanctuary of our soul, clean, bright and expectant; and receive there, through the Spirit, the call of Christ to discipleship and the life he would have us live.

FOR THE DISCUSSION GROUP

Outline

I. The concept of the Trinity.
   A. God, the Father — the Supreme Being, our Heavenly Father.
   B. God, the Holy Spirit — God as close to us as our thoughts and decisions.
   C. God, the Son — Jesus of Nazareth in whom God became incarnate.

II. More to come.
   A. During his ministry the disciples sensed Jesus' awareness of God, and also felt God's nearness.
   B. The Resurrection brought amazement and joy. The Risen Lord promised more and the disciples were expectant.
   C. The three festivals. Might *Pentecost* be the time for the coming of the Holy Spirit?

III. Pentecost.
   A. The Holy Spirit came over them.
   B. Peter's sermon and "The Day of the Lord."
   C. "Tongues As Of Fire" — Each, for himself, heard God's truth.

IV. The significance for us.
   A. Empowerment to witness.
   B. The Holy Spirit is "given to those who obey him."
   C. Peter spoke of God's judgment and mercy.
   D. The "works of the flesh" in conflict with the "fruits of the Spirit."

For Discussion

I. We believe in one God.
   A. The concept and doctrine of the Trinity fills out our comprehension of God and our experience of him.
      1. The Supreme Being and Creator of the Universe, and transcendent over all.

2. The immanence of God everywhere and in our own consciousness and conscience.
3. The historic incarnation in Jesus which is of immense importance in defining the significance of God for us human beings. The Holy Spirit bears witness to him.

II. Questions about the Holy Spirit.
   A. Was there ever a time when God did not make himself known through his Spirit in the experience of human beings? (Psalm 51: 11; John 4: 24 and many other references in the Old Testament and New Testament)
   B. Isn't the progressive revelation through the Scripture of the Old Testament and New Testament to be understood as the work of the Holy Spirit?
   C. What then was "new," following the ministry of Jesus, about the work of the Holy Spirit? (John 16:12-14; Acts 1:8; etc.)

III. Spirit-led discipleship.
   A. In what ways were the disciples different after the Day of Pentecost?
   B. How could Jesus say, "It is to your advantage that I go away"? (John 16:7)

IV. Judgment and mercy.
   A. If Peter were preaching to us today, what might he say?
   B. Does Paul speak of *judgment* when he lists the "works of the flesh" and of *mercy* when he contrasts them with the "fruit of the Spirit"? Do we find God's mercy now in his provision for a different and far better way of life to which he calls us?

The Lord's Vineyard

(Independence Day)

Read: Matthew 21:33-46; 22:15-22 and Isaiah 5:1-30

As we observe another Fourth of July let us look back across the years to rediscover and reassess our "roots" as a nation. Let us also look forward for, like the founding fathers of our country, we have faith in God and hope for the future. Just now faith and hope are in short supply, and they are not easy to have, nor to hold. Like so many today, we find it easy to be cynical and selfish. However cynicism and selfishness only add to the deep malaise we feel, and it is difficult to free ourselves from negative attitudes.

Looked at from quite a different point of view, this is a very exciting time to be a Christian and an American! Let us remember who we are and to whom — namely God himself — we are committed to serve. For us, therefore, being a Christian has much to do with being a good American; and being a good American has, for each one of us, much to do with being a Christian. The problems and dangers of the present time may, and should, increase our zest for living. With God's help we can rise to meet the challenges.

Caesar and God

When Jesus said, "Render therefore to Caesar the things that are Caesar's, and to God the things that are God's" (Matthew 22:21) he did not mean that the things which are Caesar's can be *separated* from the things that are God's but rather that we must be responsible for both. Even in that bitter world, the Roman Empire nevertheless represented civil authority and a degree of justice. Therefore when Jesus referred to "the things that are Caesar's" he was talking about *citizenship*. As his disciples today, we are called to be good citizens *and* good Christians. These two loyalties are hard-joined in our shared life as a people and as a nation.

There are many, both in and outside of our churches, who try to separate these two sides of our living. Sometimes they call it "keeping politics out of the church." Those who allege that this is what our Lord did in the incident we are considering do not understand Jesus.

Like the great prophets before him, Jesus emphasized the absolute sovereignty of God. The essence of the idea of the Kingdom of God is the overall sovereignty of the Lord. Jesus taught this in many ways, including the Great Prayer in which we are to pray again and again, "Thy kingdom come, thy will be done, on earth as it is in heaven." (Matthew 6:10) From time to time, strange ideas of the Kingdom of God are advanced but here in these words of Jesus, we have the clearest and sharpest teaching — *the Kingdom of God stands for the doing of the will of God on earth*, even as it is done above.

What God Requires of Us

Another passage that makes Jesus' teaching very clear is his parable of the Lord's Vineyard. Let us begin with a similar parable found in the fifth chapter of Isaiah. He was among the great Eighth-Century prophets. He was as clear an interpreter of the divine message concerning justice as were Amos and Hosea and he surpassed them in the sweep and majesty of his utterance. He too dared to face, with steadfast courage, the dilemmas and pressing issues confronting his people, and to focus on these, the judgment of God.

In Isaiah's ballad about the Lord's Vineyard, the teaching is very clear. God gave his people a vineyard in a fruitful place. He commanded the inhabitants to bring forth a rich harvest. Instead they produced "wild grapes." The literal translation of the Hebrew might well be "stinking fruit." God, Isaiah said, looked for justice but saw bloodshed. God heard the cry of the poor who had been robbed of their part of the inheritance by the rich and powerful. House had been joined to house and field to field until there was no room for them. And the consequences? A ruined vineyard and the judgment of the Eternal on the nation!

> "Woe to those who rise early in the
>   morning,
> that they may run after strong
>   drink,
> who tarry late into the evening
>   till wine inflames them!" (Isaiah 5:11)

> "Woe to those who call evil good
>   and good evil,
> who put darkness for light,
>   and light for darkness,
> who put bitter for sweet
>   and sweet for bitter!
> Woe to those who are wise in
>   their own eyes,
> and shrewd in their own sight!
> Woe to those who are heroes at
>   drinking wine,
> and valiant men in mixing
>   strong drink.
> Who acquit the guilty for a bribe,
>   and deprive the innocent of his right!
> Therefore, as the tongue of fire
>   devours the stubble,
> and as dry grass sinks down in
>   the flame,
> so their root will be as rotteness,
>   and their blossom go up like dust;
> for they have rejected the law of
>   the Lord of hosts,
> and have despised the word of
>   the Holy One of Israel."
>   (Isaiah 5:11, 20-24)

This was the teaching of the Prophet Isaiah more than seven hundred years before the birth of Jesus!

Our Lord Jesus made use of this same metaphor in his parable of the Vineyard. A householder, he said, planted a vineyard and made all the necessary provisions for a good harvest. The tenants were to work and return the required portion of the fruit.

"When the season of fruit drew near, he sent his servants to the tenants, to get his fruit; and the tenants took his servants and beat one, killed another, and stoned another. Again he sent other servants, more than the first; and they did the same to them. Afterward he sent his son to them, saying, 'They will respect my son.' But when the tenants saw the son, they said to themselves, 'This is the heir; come let us kill him and have his inheritance.' And they took him and cast him out of the vineyard, and killed him. When therefore the owner of the vineyard comes, what will he do to those tenants?"

Those who were listening to him answered, "He will put those wretches to a miserable death, and let out the vineyard to other tenants who will give him the fruits in their seasons." Then Jesus said,

"Therefore I tell you, the kingdom of God will be taken away from you and given to a nation producing the fruits of it." (Matthew 2:34-43)

Surely this is one of the most awesome and deeply probing statements in all Scripture. The meaning is clear. The earth, like the vineyard, is God's. The people of every nation are the tenants and are answerable to him. The fruits expected and required are integrity, righteousness, justice and reverence for God and life. God's servants are the prophetic teachers of righteousness and justice. And God's great representative is his Son, Jesus Christ!

It is a temptation to think of all this as only a reference to the great destruction that did come upon Jerusalem and Israel a few years later. But this is too easy. We cannot "get off the hook" like that! Jesus was speaking an abiding message to all nations and to all ages. He spoke a message which America needs to hear today.

America — What Kind of Vineyard Is It?

Neil Sampson, Executive Vice President of the National Association of Conservation Districts, sends a strong message to farmers and to all of us. He says that we need a new land ethic "forged of our twin concerns for the land's proper use and its proper care . . . If we value nature we will do these things and start the process soon, but if we are callous about life and measure it only by the day at hand, we will be acting the coward and the fool. In the judgment of nature this is a crowning test of our maturity and resource stewardship."*

In many areas we Americans are challenging nature itself through the exploitation and waste of exhaustible resources including the reduction of prime farm land through strip mining, urban sprawl and excessive road building; ruinous soil erosion; chemical pollution of rivers and lakes through the runoff from farms and industries; neglect of forests; and the scorning of wildlife and poaching. As an energy resource, atomic power is becoming increasingly suspect both for its ever present danger and its long lasting waste-disposal problem. It is not a pretty picture and both rural and urban people are much involved. No industry is without its greedy exploiters and state and national governmental regulations are sometimes ill-advised and sometimes blind. Over all nature itself makes the lasting judgments, and also is the great challenger. We must solve our energy needs through less dependency on expensive oil and gas, and the greater utilization of sun, wind and water power which are inexhaustible and non-polluting. We need to learn many new ways of working *with* nature, not against it.

Unto Whom Much Is Given

During the past eight years, as an interim pastor, I have served churches in Illinois and New York. I remember one beautiful summer Sunday in Rochelle, which is in the center of some of the richest farm land on earth, when I said, "If there is any place on this earth which might be thought of as God's vineyard, this is it." I said that in Illinois, and then we moved to Western New York with its vineyards and orchards, its world famous grapes, lush fruits and vegetables. Nearby was an area aptly called "Eden Valley." Both Illinois and New York are known for their great agricultural developments and their large industrial complexes, and to both states the words of Jesus must be applied, "Every one to whom much is given, of him will much be required." (Luke 12:48) I have quoted these words in Hamburg, New York; Rochelle, Rockford, Springfield, Bloomington, Paris, Quincy and Pontiac, Illinois — all lush areas of God's earth.

Making a profit is essential in any business enterprise, but in addition to making a living farmers and vegetable and fruit growers must give high consideration to feeding people in America and in other parts of the world, including the most

---

*From *The Judgment of Nature*, prepared for Soil Stewardship Week, May 11-18, 1980.

impoverished areas. Likewise, the industrialists and unions, merchants and professional people must serve basic human needs. When profits, high salaries, fees and wages are given the greatest consideration, inflation and recession inevitably follow. A bloated economy will eventually die of its own obesity. This is today's lesson which must be learned. And only through the discharge of the high responsibility of service to others can anyone's life and work be squared with the Christian ethic.

What a vineyard is all about us! The challenge is great, indeed; and the opportunity and joy of Christian witness is unlimited. All of us have an important job to do for and in the future of God's vineyard, beginning right here in America where we live.

FOR THE DISCUSSION GROUP

Outline

I. A challenging time to be a Christian and an American.
   A. Called to be good citizens and good Christians. Consideration of two of Jesus' most important teachings.
   B. Isaiah's ballad of the Lord's Vineyard and Jesus' Parable.
   C. "The kingdom of God will be taken away from you and given to a nation producing the fruits of it."

II. America — what kind of vineyard is it?
   A. The judgment of nature.
   B. Both rural and urban people are much involved.
   C. Learning new ways of working with nature.

III. "Unto whom much is given."
   A. Great agricultural and industrial complexes.
   B. Beyond profits, serving human needs.
   C. Unlimited opportunity and responsibility.

For Discussion

I. Faith and hope, now in short supply.
   A. How may we free ourselves from negative attitudes?
   B. Did Jesus mean to separate the things of Caesar and God? Why do so many wish to do this?
   C. Study Isaiah's ballad of the Lord's Vineyard. At how many points does this ancient "judgment" apply to us?
   D. In what ways does Jesus' parable differ from Isaiah's ballad?

II. Working against nature?
   A. Through the exploitation and waste of exhaustible resources?
   B. Through soil erosion?
   C. Through chemical pollution?
   D. Through neglect?
   E. Through atomic waste-disposal?

III. Working with nature.
   A. How practical is this idea?
   B. Can essential human needs today be met without exploitation of natural resources?

C. Will nature make the final judgment?
IV. Profits vs. service.
   A. Have these two gotten out of workable balance?
   B. How dearly must we now pay?
      Who will pay first and most?
   C. What is our Christian witness?

Can a Rich Man Get into Heaven?

Read: Matthew 19:16-26

Not long ago a Religious News Service article entitiled, "Does God Prefer the Poor Above All Others?" appeared in our Sunday papers. It is a timely and important subject, especially in view of the world hunger situation. As I began to prepare this message I realized that I had undertaken a large and difficult subject. At one point it occurred to me that I might really make a sensation (that I might even make the front page of the newspaper!) if I were to stand here and declare that "No rich man *can* get into heaven!"

Well . . . I am not going to say this. Some of the finest people, and some of the finest Christians, I have known have been rich people. However, beyond this, and beyond all personal judgments, I remember that although men look on the outward appearance, and form favorable and unfavorable impressions, the Lord looks into the heart of each one. (1 Samuel 16:7)

The Biblical record, and especially the teachings and actions of Jesus, help us to understand as clearly as we may, how God does see all of us. And the question, "Can a rich man get into heaven?" does carry us into some deep soul-searching. What did Jesus mean when, in the Sermon on the Mount, he said, "No one can serve two masters . . . You cannot serve God and Mammon"? (Matthew 6:24) *Mammon* means covetousness, greed and the passion for acquiring and hoarding riches. Are any of us guilty of this?

The Rich Young Ruler

The nineteenth chapter of Matthew records the incident of the rich young ruler who came to Jesus and asked, "Teacher, what good deed must I do, to have eternal life?" (Matthew 19:16) On the face of it, he was simply asking, "What good thing can I do to get a ticket to heaven?" The thinking of many people is hardly more mature than this. In fact, this very New Testament story has given rise to countless jokes about St. Peter weighing a person's "good deeds" at the pearly gates.

In the Biblical story, Jesus took the young man seriously and said, "Keep the commandments." Thinking on a superficial level, the young man asked, "Which?" Jesus, still taking him seriously, and leading him further, said, "You shall not kill, You shall not commit adultery, You shall not steal, You shall not bear false witness, Honor your father and mother, and, You shall love your neighbor as yourself." (Matthew 19:18-19) To this the rich young man boastfully replied, "All these I have observed" (all these . . . perfectly?) And then, perhaps sensing a lack in his life, and the very thing which caused him to inquire of Jesus, in the first place, he said, "What do I still lack?" (Matthew 19:20)

Mark tells us that as Jesus looked at him, he loved him. (Mark 10:21) This can only mean that Jesus saw good qualities and a fine potentiality in him. Wanting to lead him on toward a better understanding and commitment, Jesus then said, "Go, sell what you possess and give to the poor, and you will have treasure in heaven; and come, follow me." (Matthew 19:21) In this way the young man was confronted with the issues of life, and *challenged to be a disciple.* In such a personal way Jesus challenged all who came sincerely, and he still does. We do not need to suppose that Jesus wanted this man to become a penniless beggar on the street, but to make a searching of his soul and life. In essence he said to him, if you come, you must come on my terms, not your superficial thinking and selfish wishes. You have much to learn!

We read that Jesus' invitation was not accepted; that the young man "went away sorrowful, for he had great possessions!" (Matthew 19:22) Then turning to some of the disciples who had witnessed what had happened, Jesus said to them, "It will be hard for a rich man to enter the kingdom of Heaven . . . it is easier for a camel to go through the eye of a needle than for a rich man to enter the Kingdom of God." (Matthew 19:24) It is not easy for us today to understand this statement. However it is quite clear that it cannot be taken literally for it is impossible for a camel to pass through the eye of a needle! Indeed, it is *ludicrous;* and this is the best way to regard it! There are other examples when Jesus spoke in flashing hyperbole, especially when he wanted to drive home an unpopular truth. Centuries later Abraham Lincoln did the same thing. An hyperbole is an exaggeration or overstatement intended to produce an effect, without it being taken literally. Elton Trueblood, in his book on *The Humor of Jesus* lists thirty such humorous passages in the Gospels. Also in the rabbinical literature of the time, there are many illustrations of such humor.

We may suppose that the disciples understood and chuckled over the absurd picture of a big camel, humps and all, squeezing through the tiny eye of a needle; and then, almost as quickly, becoming quite serious as indeed Jesus intended them to be. The truth came home to them and they asked, "Who then can be saved?" Jesus' answer is much more penetrating than at first we may think. *"With men it is impossible, but with God, all things are possible."* (Matthew 19:26) In other words, but for the grace of God (that is, the help of God) no one can stand up to the temptations of avarice, dollar-madness, covetousness, greed and the passion to acquire things and hoard riches.

Christian Discipleship

Christian discipleship is not easy. If we really come to Christ, we come, not on our own terms but his, and they are particularized for each one of us.

This is the lesson of the Parable of the Talents. There are the five-talented person, the two-talented person and the one-talented person, and each has his own set of abilities and opportunities. No two persons are exactly alike, but there is equality of all on the level of responsibility to make the best use of what each one has. In the parable those who used and developed what they had were praised and rewarded, but the one who did nothing was condemned and lost what he had.

Among Jesus' followers were some well-to-do persons. Among these were those whom many people in that day — and some even today — would least expect Jesus to call, and even less, to become followers. Think of some of them.

The first four to be called among the Twelve Apostles were Simon Peter and Andrew his brother; and James and John the sons of Zebedee. (Matthew 4:18-22) These four men, and quite likely their fathers before them, were partners in a fishing business at the Sea of Galilee. We have no way of knowing what their bank accounts were but it seems likely that they were not poor but owned their own equipment and paid their "hired servants." As disciples of Jesus they came to the point of giving him their highest loyalty but there is reason to think that they retained, at least for a time, their business interests and connections. When, however, it became necessary for them to make a choice between fishing and "fishing for men" (that is, doing the work to which they were called by their risen Lord), they chose to follow him. (John, Chapter 21)

There was Zacchaeus, a rich tax collector whose heart and life were changed. To the amazement of all, especially the self-righteous Pharisees, Jesus went to his house. We are informed that Zacchaeus promised to give half of his goods to the poor and to restore fourfold to anyone he had defrauded. The record is very brief and we wish that we had the answer to many questions, but we do know this: Jesus said to Zacchaeus, "Today salvation has come to this house" and referring to his own ministry, he added, "The Son of man came to seek and save the lost." (Luke 19:1-10)

In the presence of our Lord, this man learned that there are searching questions to be answered as to how money is made and spent. The Christian goal and standard is true human service, *not* maximum profits without regard for honesty or the hurt of others. If one's occupation makes no real contribution to the welfare of others, should a Christian engage in it? Of course, "the welfare of others" covers a great many things, but the guiding principle is clear. Honest work on a farm or in a factory, or in a store or office, or in a schoolroom, or anywhere else needs to be adequately and fairly compensated, but a still greater concern is: How may this work help or injure others — especially those in the greatest need?

In the Gospel of Luke and in Acts, there are a number of references to women who contributed "out of their means" to Jesus' ministry and mission. (Luke 8:3) Some of these continued among his followers from Galilee through his crucifixion and resurrection, and into the new Christian community. Even in that male-dominated society there were well-to-do and independent women. Among them were a number of the most devoted and conscientious followers of our Lord.

There was Nicodemus, a man of wealth and a member of the Jewish Sanhedrin who inquired of Jesus by night and received from him the important teaching about the need to be "born again." (John 3:1-8) His was the lone voice in the Sanhedrin to question the obvious prejudice against Jesus (John 7:50-52). There was Joseph of Arimathea, another wealthy man, who, at considerable personal peril, saw to Jesus' burial with deep respect and devotion. (John 19:38-42)

From the day of Jesus' earthly ministry to the present, some of his most committed and able followers have been persons of wealth and power. Nevertheless, there is abundant evidence of the need for Jesus' warning of the deceitfulness of riches. (Mark 4:19) And we must never forget Jesus' compassion and concern for the poor. Liberation theology is clearly in evidence throughout the New Testament.

The Poor

The article in the newspaper with which we began emphasized the growing awareness of all religious groups, in the Judeo-Christian tradition, of God's concern for the poor and, as followers of Jesus, our legitimate concern. It spoke of Archbishop Oscar A. Romero of El Salvador who championed the cause of the poor in his country and who, for this very reason, was murdered at the altar of his church. It spoke of Mother Teresa of Calcutta, the Nobel Prize winner. It spoke of the Protestant and Orthodox Churches, represented in the World Council of Churches. It told of the new position of concern for the poor of earth now being shown by the Evangelical churches in America and around the world. Also it might well have quoted the Pope's words spoken during his recent visits abroad.

Time and time again we see it on the evening network news: some of the saddest and most terrible pictures we will ever see. I recall seeing untold numbers of babies and mothers suffering and dying of starvation! It was mind-boggling and heart-rending. The pictures were taken in Africa but it could well have been in Cambodia, or in parts of Latin America.

No reader of the New Testament can fail to see the Mind of Christ coming to bear upon the vast poverty, hunger and death in many parts of the world today. In spite of all difficulties, we Christians in affluent America must hear and heed the Master's call to us more clearly and definitely. That call must challenge our whole commitment of mind, heart and will, as well as our money and our possessions. We must let Christ control our very way of life!

Who Then Can Be Saved?

Who then can be saved? Not the rich man, nor the poor man,

per se but those whose heart, mind and life have been changed and who, therefore, really choose to come under the control of our Lord. How is such a thing possible? The answer is, as it has always been, *"only by the grace of God!"*

FOR THE DISCUSSION GROUP

Outline

I. This question carries us into deep soul-searching.
   A. "You cannot serve God and Mammon." Are any of us guilty of trying to do this?

II. The rich young ruler.
   A. His question: How may I get into heaven?
   B. Jesus challenged him to become a disciple.
   C. "It is easier for a camel to go through the eye of a needle..."
   D. "Who then can be saved?"
   E. "With God, all things are possible."

III. Discipleship.
   A. Coming on Christ's terms, not ours.
   B. The Parable of the Talents.
   C. Among Jesus' followers there were several well-to-do persons mentioned:
      1. Among the Twelve
      2. Zacchaeus
      3. Some women
      4. Nicodemus
      5. Joseph of Arimathea

IV. Jesus' compassion and concern for the poor.
   A. Many persons of wealth and power were among the disciples; but there is much evidence of the need for Jesus' warning concerning the deceitfulness of riches.
   B. Clearly Jesus had compassion and concern for the poor.
   C. Appalling poverty, hunger and suffering, an immense twentieth century problem.
   D. In affluent America we need Christ to change and control our way of life.

V. Only by the grace of God!

For Discussion

I. A timely subject in view of world hunger and the economic situation.

II. The interview and what followed.
   A. Consider the commandments which Jesus chose to emphasize. Which of the Ten did he omit? Which one did he add? Does this suggest that Jesus was addressing this man's particular need?
   B. Discuss Jesus' use of hyperbole. Suggest some present-day examples.
   C. Discuss the disciples' amazement and question.
   D. Discuss, in depth, Jesus' answer.

III. The deceitfulness of riches.
   A. How many rich people are aware of the danger? If possible, give examples of those who are.
   B. How are attitudes and actions affected by wealth and position? What is it that causes some rich people to act — and react — quite differently from other well-to-do people?
   C. Discuss how covetousness affects everyone. How may we cope with it?

IV. The liberation of the "haves" and the "have-nots."
   A. Do people who have much, need to be "liberated" from selfishness?
   B. Did Jesus have compassion for the "poor rich"? Is this among the reasons Jesus went to the home of Zacchaeus, invited Matthew to be one of the Twelve, and counseled Nicodemus?
   C. May involvement of the "haves" with the "have-nots" work out for the liberation of both? What does it take *on both sides* for this to happen?

V. Discipleship on Christ's terms, not ours, makes the difference.

Our Two Incomes

Read: Haggai 1:5-6,9; Luke 12:13-21; 14:28-30

"*You have looked for much, and, lo it came to little.*" These are the words of the Old Testament Prophet Haggai as he rebuked the people, and set them again to work rebuilding the Temple of the Lord. Hear more of what he said: "Consider how you have fared. You have sown much, and harvested little; you eat, but you never have enough; you drink, but you never have your fill; you clothe yourselves, but no one is warm; and he who earns wages earns wages to put them into a bag with holes . . . You have looked for much, and, lo, it came to little." (Haggai 1:5-6,9)

As we read these words do we not feel that Haggai is speaking to us? With inflation what it is today do we not feel as though we put our earnings into a bag with holes in it? Perhaps we even feel this way about our Christian experience and life itself.

Church Membership — How Rewarding Is It?

Across the years, as a pastor, I have shared in the welcoming of many hundreds of people into church membership. During my fifteen years as the pastor of the First Presbyterian Church in Bay City, Michigan, some 1800 persons united with the church. In Lincoln, Nebraska, where I was pastor of the Westminster Presbyterian Church, with a membership of some 2400, it was necessary to receive about 125 persons each year just to hold our own numerically. For some time now, we have been living in a highly mobile society.

It was a privilege to work with so many people and to be their pastor. I conducted "New Member Classes" four or five times a year. These helped the new people to better understand what church membership is all about, and to become acquainted with other members. And now, in my interim pastorates, I always try to reach out to new people.

It is my observation that a large majority of those who unite with a church do it sincerely and with the hope that they will both receive and share in something very good. *I have seen the expectations of many largely fulfilled!* They have experienced the joy and the strength of the Christian life, and they were glad to be fruitful members of the church in the community it served. But, alas, I have also observed all too many members who get very little out of their membership and, after a time, become indifferent and entirely inactive. They "looked for much, and lo, it came to little."

The joy of a pastor's ministry is found, to a large extent, in relationship to and with this first group, that is, with those who get a great deal out of their Christian faith and church membership. Conversely, the disappointments of the pastorate come, to a large degree, in connection with the second group. The frustrations and disappointments of these members also become the frustrations and disappointments of their pastor, and quite properly a burden on him — for they too are "his people"!

What makes the difference between these two groups? Obviously there are many individual factors; and we must never speak casually or simplistically about anyone. However, there are clues in two of Jesus' parables.

The Tower Builder and the Rich Farmer

In one of them our Lord said, "Which of you, desiring to build a tower, does not first sit down and count the cost, whether he has enough to complete it? Otherwise, when he has laid a foundation, and is not able to finish, all who see it begin to mock him, saying, 'This man began to build, and was not able to finish.' " (Luke 14:28-30) Not counting the cost is all too often the problem. Many learn the hard way about the folly of trying to live beyond their financial means. Sooner or later the loan company or bank stands at the door to repossess the TV or the car or even the house . . . and with it, the way of life.

Something very much like this can happen on a large scale and becomes what we call a recession or depression. No country can indefinitely take from and squander more than it puts into its productive processes. America, and many other parts of the world, have neglected the basis of a viable economy. This is why we now hear the urgent and widespread call for "reindustrialization." The nation's productive capacity must be rebuilt and people must get back to work producing and providing *essential* goods and services. For a time nations, like individuals, may try to deceive even themselves by a pretense of strength which is simply not there. Basic human and material resources may remain but if they are not used as they should be, there can only be trouble — big trouble.

There is a remarkable parallel between economics and spiritual reality. *Trying to live beyond one's spiritual production, and income, also becomes impossible.*

Consider another of Jesus' parables. The farmer in this story saw his security only in material wealth. Jesus said, "The land of a rich man brought forth plentifully; and he thought to himself, 'What shall I do, for I have nowhere to store my crops?' And he said, 'I will do this: I will pull down my barns, and build larger ones; and there I will store all my grain and my goods. And I will say to my soul, Soul, you have ample goods laid up for many years; take your ease, eat, drink, be merry.' But God said to him, 'Fool! This night your soul is required of you; and the things you have prepared, whose will they be?' " Then Jesus added, "So is he who lays up treasure for himself, and is not rich toward God." (Luke 12:16-21) *Alas, he had hoped for much, and had accumulated much, but little came of it.* He had lived far beyond his spiritual income.

One's Spiritual Income

What does it mean to have a spiritual income? And how may one have it? Well, it isn't easy! Although it comes in quite a different way, one's spiritual income is harder and more taxing to secure than is the getting of an adequate financial income.

Jesus made it clear that there is far more to discipleship than learning to feel good about oneself. In the end it takes all that we have and all that we are. In the Sermon on the Mount, he said, "Enter by the narrow gate; for the gate is wide and the way is easy, that leads to destruction, and those who enter by it are many. For the gate is narrow and the way is hard, that leads to life, and those who find it are few." (Matthew 7:13-14) The discipline of oneself is required. Nothing in anyone's life ever comes easily. Ignace Jan Paderewski, the world-renowned Polish pianist and statesman, at the height of his career, practiced many hours every day on his beloved instrument. He said, "If I miss practicing one day, I know it. If I miss two days, those around me know it. If I miss three days, the whole world knows it." Such is the "narrow gate" in music, in sports, in professional skills, and in many other areas of life, and *in one's devotion to God and the things of his Kingdom.*

SPIRITUAL INCOME IS THE RECEIVING OF DIVINE GRACE. IT BECOMES MANIFEST IN THE WITNESS TO GOD'S WILL IN ONE'S PERSONAL LIFE, AND IN RELATIONSHIPS WITH OTHERS.

Some years ago, I received a candid letter from a young man who had attended our church a few times. In it he said, "I am young and facing the confusing problems in this materialistic world where the blind are leading the blind. I am rotating on a sensual axis. Every day I am filled up with greed, hate, burning passion, and sex. Wherever I work, greed for the other man's job and salary is dominating. In the newspapers I read about murders, robberies, rape, threats of war, etc. When I walk down the street and scrutinize the theater displays I see photos of the latest sex sensation . . . Are you strong enough to change my world? One hundred and sixty-seven hours a week I am tempted to yield to sensuality. One hour a week I am told why I should not yield to it."

The key sentence in this letter is, "*Are you strong enough to change my world?*" My answer to him was: "Of course, I am not! No minister or church ever makes such a claim. The Christian teaching is utterly different. It is, 'You will seek me and find me; when you seek me with all your heart.' (Jeremiah 29:13) If we really want and expect God to transform our lives, he can and he will. But we must be willing and anxious to turn from self-will to God's will; we must learn his will and seek by his grace to do it."

Too many people do not want or expect their religion to change them. They think vaguely of their church connection in terms of it doing something *for* them (indeed, even in spite of them) whereas the great accomplishments of faith are always *in* and *through* the lives of those who deeply and sincerely want the help, the grace of God.

This young man who wrote to me did not appreciate the fact that Christians have always lived in a sinful world and that love and honor have never been easy to achieve or hold. He did not understand the necessity of experiencing God's grace through Jesus Christ — the great divine help from beyond — the help which only God can give.

He spoke of being subjected 167 hours a week to temptations and only one hour a week — in church — to God. Did this mean that he never reads the Bible or prays? Did this mean that he never reads good literature or listens to inspiring music or watches the better programs on TV? Did this mean that he never takes time to associate with good people and work along with them in church and community service? Did this mean that he did nothing, and wants to do nothing, to have an adequate spiritual income?

The basis of God's promise is quite different and Paul makes it clear in these words: "Just as sin ruled by means of death, so also God's grace rules by means of righteousness, leading us to eternal life through Jesus Christ our Lord." (Romans 5:21 TEV)

The Source of Our Incomes

Finally, let it be noted that the ultimate *Source* of both our financial and spiritual incomes is God. We have to work for them but their origin and continuing foundation are beyond us. We cannot produce even one slice of bread all by ourselves. There are the sun, seed, soil, air and rain but without the farmer, the miller and the baker there would be no bread. God has made it so that the minds, hearts and wills of many people, in addition to their hands, are required in the production of food. This means that many types of discipline are needed — mental, spiritual and physical — and must be renewed and continued day after day. It is in this way that God gives us our bread and a vast number of other good things. Likewise we have our spiritual income only as we are good stewards of all that inspires us through our own work, the work of others and most of all God's amazing grace which we do not merit and can only accept, and be deeply grateful. God is in the whole creative process, *and so are we!* Our prayers do not lessen what we must do but rather greatly increase our perception of our own stewardship responsibilities in it.

Bishop Edwin Holt Hughes of the Methodist Church was preaching in a rural church. In his sermon, he said that we hold our property only as stewards of the divine *Owner*. Later at Sunday dinner, the farmer who was entertaining him said, quite critically, "Do you really mean to suggest that I don't own this land which is my farm?" Looking at the farmer, the Bishop replied, "Ask me that question a hundred years from now!"

The idea of stewardship, when it is comprehended, is far more inspiring than the idea of ownership of a farm or anything else. We don't need, certainly, to wait a hundred years to know the answer to the farmer's question. However, we do need to let

God speak to us much more clearly and sharply concerning the use of our time, abilities, money, personal example and total influence. We must spend our material and spiritual incomes. We must invest them in the lives of others. We must use and give them wisely to the glory of God in and through the church.

Praise God from Whom All Blessings Flow!

FOR THE DISCUSSION GROUP

Outline

I. Haggai's rebuke.
   A. It seems as though he was speaking to us.

II. Church membership — how rewarding is it?
   A. "I have seen high expectations fulfilled; also where they were not."
   B. Joy and disappointments for both pastors and members.
   C. What makes the difference?
      Parable of the Tower Builder.

III. Folly in not counting the cost.
   A. Economic recession sets in.
   B. Living beyond our spiritual production and income also leads to disaster.
      Parable of the Rich Farmer.

IV. One's spiritual income.
   A. What it takes.
   B. What it is.
   C. A young man's letter.

V. Our two incomes, financial and spiritual, come from God.
   A. God is in the whole creative process, *and so are we*.
   B. We are called to be stewards of both incomes to the glory of God.

For Discussion

I. Unrealized expectations.
   A. Why? What can we do?

II. Don't lower expectations; realize them!
   A. What do we have a right to expect in church membership? Make a comprehensive list.
   B. If there are disappointments, how much of the "blame" should go to the pastor, other members, and oneself?
   C. How may we all better become a part of the "people of God" in today's world?

III. A viable economy.
   A. Is it possible to take out more than is produced without disaster? Are the consequences inflation and recession?
   B. Is there a parallel in one's spiritual "production" and "income"?
   C. What was the Rich Farmer's mistake? Was he thinking only of what he might get and hold for himself? Was he blind to his stewardship responsibilities? Did he neglect his spiritual income?

IV. What must we do to have a steady and growing spiritual income?
   A. Study the young man's letter. How accurate is his description of today's world? What did he reveal about himself when he asked, "Are you strong enough to change my world?"
   B. How many want the church or the minister to do something "good" for them without in any way changing their ways of thinking or living?
   C. Discuss the teaching, "You will seek me and find me; when you seek me with all your heart." Have we discovered this great promise of God to be true in our own lives?

V. In what ways should and could our stewardship determine our two incomes?

Work and Life — Life and Work

(Labor Day)
Read: Galatians 5:25-6:10 and Ephesians 4:1

The strike of the hard-pressed Polish workers has been much in the recent news. Not long ago, a prominent Polish emigre in London exclaimed, "If Karl Marx were alive today, he could not believe his eyes!" *Time* magazine put this statement in perspective. It commented, ". . . the father of modern Communism would have been astonished by the spectacle: a socialist country whose ports, factories and mills were crippled by an industrial revolt of its own angry workers; and a Communist Party leader abjectly confessing his regime's economic failure and dependence on capitalist banking consortiums for life-saving loans. Most incredible of all to the man who contemptuously dismissed religion as 'the opiate of the people' would have been the sight of thousands of strikers and their families kneeling at the gates of a shipyard, praying and singing hymns before the flower-bedecked portrait of a Polish Pope." (*Time* September 1, 1980) So it is that we watch and marvel at the changing world scene.

Our Labor Day is still important on the American calendar. It reminds us of significant developments in our history as a people and as a nation, and it points to serious current problems. Let us see this morning what this day can mean for us personally, and in the context of Christian commitment. Let us begin with work and life.

Work and Life

While some of us, secure in our employment and/or income, are in a holiday mood, there are many around us who are unemployed, underemployed or apprehensive over the possibility of losing their jobs. As we all know, work and income are important for peace of mind. But if we have never been unemployed for a considerable length of time, we can scarcely appreciate what that can mean. Conversely, if we have never been employed and have little likelihood of ever getting a real job we can scarcely imagine what it is like to be in *that* situation. Let us, therefore, on this or any other Labor Day, try to feel something of the benumbing pain in the lives of young people and older people who have no work, whether it is their fault or not.

In 597 B.C., after King Nebuchadnezzar captured Jerusalem, Ezekiel, who was both a priest and prophetic teacher, was taken to Telabib on the banks of the river Chebar. There, among the Hebrew captives in Babylon, he learned of the conditions under which his fellow countrymen lived. Later he wrote, "And I sat where they sat, and remained there astonished among them seven days." (Ezekiel 3:15 KJV) Most of us are quite isolated from those unlike ourselves — racially, culturally and economically. This becomes obvious as we consider other parts of the world, and other people even in our own country. We may be unaware of what conditions may exist in our own neighborhood, or next door. Christians are those who try to sit where others sit in order that they may know, care about and love them.

Any honest job is better than no job at all, and, at present, many people are in no position to be choosy. We admire anyone who makes the most of whatever work he has and builds upon it. Many fantastic careers have begun at the bottom, through honesty, hard work, improving the product or service and thereby contributing to the success of the business or undertaking. For any kind of lasting satisfaction, it is important to know that whatever we do, it contributes directly or indirectly to the welfare of others.

I am reminded of the reporter who talked with three men who, with many others, were excavating a good sized area. Of each he asked, "What are you doing?" The first two answered disgustedly, "I am digging a hole, can't you see?" But the third workman answered, "I am building a cathedral!" How important it is to find the "cathedral" in every job!

Even if our work, in itself, does not seem to make much

contribution to the good of others, it nevertheless enables us to live, and live creatively for family, church, community, special individuals, causes, etc. Years ago, in St. Louis, in my first pastorate, there was a lonely postman who worked hard, at low pay delivering mail (an obviously important function) and who gave much time to his church and was one of its largest contributors. Some who perhaps were made uncomfortable by the size of his gifts thought that the officers should inform him that he need not give so much. Fortunately wiser and kindlier members understood how much his commitment to Christ and the church meant to him, and quietly showed their appreciation for what he did.

Such may be the relationship between one's work and one's life and it is very good.

Life and Work

However, a different orientation is possible: *Not work to provide a living, but our life expressing itself through a carefully chosen and developed vocation.* Let us call this not "Work and Life" but "Life and Work." Here a person's work is more than the means of making a living; it is in and of itself a source of satisfaction and significant accomplishment. Many thinkers have made and stressed the possibility for this greater value in one's work. It is a serious mistake to suppose that we must work only for money which then may be spent for the real interests and satisfactions of life. Emerson once said of such money that "it costs too much." Work should be not only a way of earning a living but also the way to live a rich, interesting and creative life.

Today, very unfortunately, the test of almost everything has become *the dollar sign!* Nothing can cheapen life more. It is commonly made the "bottom line," but it isn't. To prove this, one has only to look with some discernment at the passing scene (this morning's newspaper or newscast), and also to look within his own soul. It used to be that men and women would cherish a college education for the personal enrichment it would bring to them, and how it might also enable them to serve others in a business or profession. This is still true for some. But for many, unfortunately, a college education is simply a way of getting a job that pays more money. A college education today seems less likely to provide an inclusive and penetrating outlook on life. It fails to confront the student with Immanuel Kant's three questions: What can I know? What ought I do? What may I hope?

By narrowing its perspective to "the bottom line" of material gain, a college education has lost much of its true potentiality and value. Money can buy things — an abundance of them — but "things" have a way of losing their significance. Money can buy power and prestige but these, unless there is a lot of character and high purpose to go along with them, easily lead to dishonesty, corruption and disgrace. Money cannot buy personal integrity, true friends, peace of mind, health or lasting respect.

Some of the happiest moments in my ministry have come when talking with young people about their vocations. If and when we get past "How much money can I get?", we come into a different perspective entirely. We talk about personal interests and abilities, human needs and the future of our country, and the kind of associations we really want with others, and may have with them, along the road ahead.

A youth, who had been in one of my confirmation classes and was now soon to graduate from high school, sat across the desk from me and asked, "Do you think that I could be another Albert Schweitzer?" Knowing of his very unusual scholastic ability and his high commitment, I said, "Yes, if this is the way God is calling you and if you put yourself to it!" I followed his career through the University of Michigan and beyond. He did study both medicine and theology and became a research medical scientist and physician, and also has devoted himself through the years to Christ and the church.*

As a young man, I was a member of a church in which some thirty of us chose to enter the ordained ministry. It was not an authoritarian-type church. Our pastor encouraged us to do our own thinking and to make our own decisions. One of the evaluations every congregation should face is just this: How many of our young men and women have heard and heeded Christ's call to serve professionally in his church? Of course, not all Christians can or should be employed church workers but some out of every congregation should feel so led.

Our Response

Work and Life, Life and Work. At whichever point we begin or wherever we are now, we should hear Paul saying to the Church in Ephesus and to us: "I . . . beg you to lead a life worthy of the calling to which you have been called." (Ephesians 4:1) "Calling" is another word for "vocation," but *calling* is more inclusive. It

---

*This "youth" has become a world famous medical researcher and physician. He is Dr. Richard D. Stewart of Racine, Wisconsin who directs fifty medical units worldwide.

includes all that we have, and all that we are!

We speak of a minister being "called" to the pastorate of a church, and we hope and pray that the one called is the one God wants in that pulpit and in that position. However, God calls every one of us! This is the awesome truth whether we like it or not, and whether we accept it or not. The Bible is full of accounts of those called, and stories of what happened when they obeyed or disobeyed. Likewise, history records countless stories of those who were faithful or unfaithful.

In every family circle, in every community and in every congregation, life stories of men and women, and their work and accomplishments are written into the lives of others. What kind of record are we now making? With God's help, what kind of record may we yet make?

FOR THE DISCUSSION GROUP

Outline

I. Polish workers' strike.
   A. Labor Day is important on the American calendar.

II. Work and life.
   A. Identifying with others.
   B. Making the most of whatever work one has. Finding the "Cathedral" in every job.
   C. Living creatively. An illustration.

III. Life and work.
   A. Here let us see life expressing itself through a chosen and developed vocation.
   B. It is a serious mistake to work only for money.
   C. Realizing the potentiality and value of a college education.
   D. Vocational counseling. An illustration.

IV. On being called.
   A. In every congregation some should feel the call to professional church service.
   B. Calling a new pastor.
   C. God calls everyone of us!

For Discussion

I. Organizing workers vs. communism.
   A. Labor Day reminds us of significant developments in our history.

II. Christian empathy.
   A. How far are we willing to go in sharing the "hurt" others feel?
   B. How may we and others make the most of any type of honest work?
   C. Discuss ways of making life more useful and satisfying beyond one's employment.

III. Choosing, preparing for and developing one's vocation.
   A. Here work is more than making a living; it becomes a source of satisfaction and significant accomplishment.

How important is this? Is preparation for such a vocation worth much time and effort?
- B. How can the "bottom line" dollar cheapen life?
- C. Among a multitude of college courses, experiences and opportunities how may today's student find his or her way?

IV. God's call to each of us.
- A. Discuss Paul's urgent appeal to the Christians in Ephesus, "I . . . beg you to lead a life worthy of the calling to which you have been called." Should the members of every congregation say this to one another and especially to their young people?
- B. Should each church have special programs on vocational choice? Should such programs be concerned with more than church vocations?
- C. Should experienced men and women give time to young people in choosing and developing their vocations?

Instead of the Thorn

(An Interpretation of God's Judgment and Mercy)
Read: Isaiah 55

White Pines State Park is one of the most beautiful and restful places in northern Illinois. One evening, during our interim pastorate in Rockford, we had dinner at the fine restaurant there. We sat at a table by a window and enjoyed the good food and relaxed in the natural beauty all around. Looking up from the place where I was seated my eyes rested upon a large picture which was on sale by a local artist. It caught and held the attention of all who saw it. It was a painting of a large round object obviously representing the world. Everywhere in it were human faces, indeed, a whole collage of faces representative of every race and nationality. All of these people were tightly bound by steel bands while through them were thousands of spikes, like great thorns, which pierced their faces or bodies and extended through the whole earth. It was a horrible but a graphic representation of *Tortured Humanity*.

At first I resented such a picture in a dining room in a beautiful state park where I had gone "to get away from it all." This, however, was only a passing reaction. Why not be reminded of the real world of human sin and suffering in the midst of God's also very real world of natural beauty and the renewal of life? Even as I sat there looking at this picture, this message was born as I thought of the words from the fifty-fifth chapter of Isaiah:

"Instead of the thorn shall come up
    the cypress;
  instead of the brier shall come
    up the myrtle;
and it shall be to the Lord for a
    memorial,
  for an everlasting sign which
    shall not be cut off." (Isaiah 55:13)

What thorns we plant in our lives! As I work with people and see the unnecessary trouble into which they get themselves, I say over and over again to myself, and sometimes to them, *Why?* . . . so obviously wrong, unnecessary and disastrous, why? And think of the thorns which we plant in our relationships with others. How needless they are! How harmful! Having implanted some thorns — and even some spikes — are we too proud to withdraw them? Do we choose to go on hurting and being hurt rather than admitting our mistakes, our unkindnesses, and our sins against God and others? *In such anguish, which may become great indeed, we see the judgment of God.*

"For my thoughts are not your
    thoughts,
  neither are your ways my ways
    says the Lord." (Isaiah 55:8)

The Thorn and the Myrtle

The thorn is the fiercely growing wild bush which is still found in the Jordan Valley, and through the wilderness and even close to Jerusalem. It forms impenetrable clumps of savage, tearing thorns. (Was it from one of these bushes that the crown of thorns was made and then brutally pushed down on Jesus' head as the soldiers mocked and beat him before he was crucified?)

One the other hand, myrtle is one of the most highly prized and widely distributed growths in all Palestine. In poor soils it is a shrub, but in good soil it rises to considerable size as a bushy tree. It has dark green scented leaves, starry white flowers, and dark berries which may be eaten. In the thought of the Hebrew poet, it was a symbol of God's everlasting providence and the hope in the human heart without which we perish.

The Three "Isaiahs"

A careful study of Isaiah, the twenty-third book in the Old

Testament, indicates that it is not the work of one writer but of three who lived and spoke in different but succeeding periods of Hebrew history. Chapters 1-39 reflect the history beginning about 738 B.C.; chapters 40-55 relate to the period about a century and a half later; and chapters 56-66 came from approximately 50 to 100 years later.

The writer of chapters 40 through 55 is unknown but is identified as the Second Isaiah. He is regarded by many Biblical scholars as the greatest poet and prophetic teacher in Hebrew History. After Cyrus conquered Babylon in 538 B.C. and the Jewish exiles were freed to return to Judah, he spoke to them, and through them to the nation. His message was full of hope and comfort. With profound spiritual insight and unshaken faith he met the great disaster which had come upon his nation. He had a true sense of the epic nature of his people and of their significance in the divine plan.

In the fifty-fifth chapter of Isaiah, the Second Isaiah brings his message to a climax. It merits careful and extended study. In the last verse, he spoke of the Lord's memorial or everlasting sign. This makes us think of the ancient kings who had inscriptions made and left throughout their realms, attesting to their greatness. Perhaps he was thinking of Sennacherib, Nebuchadnezzar and Cyrus. The pyramids of Egypt are the most amazing examples, but every country has its "historic markers." What sort of an inscription or sign does the Lord of all have in human history? This is the question to which the Second Isaiah addresses himself. His answer is as mind-stretching as it is wonderful. He saw the sign which the Eternal has written across history to be the rebirth, the recurrence of faith and hope, of goodness and mercy in the hearts and lives of people! This is his profound declaration of faith.

All Are Summoned and Welcomed

There is an old saying that "hope springs eternal." But it doesn't, at least not by itself. Our times need much more than "whistling to keep from being afraid." Many of today's turned-off youths also need much more than this if they are not to permanently remain "marginal" people. Discouragement comes to those in every age bracket. When we feel the downward pull of pessimism and hopelessness, which at times "grabs" all of us, it is good to look back some 2500 years and ponder again the thinking of one of the greatest Old Testament prophets. What really was his message? *All are summoned for the renewal of hope by God himself.*

> "Ho, everyone who thirsts,
>   come to the waters;
> and he who has no money,
>   come, buy and eat!
> Come, buy wine and milk
>   without money and without price." (Isaiah 55:1)

Here the people are called to come and seek spiritual nourishment symbolized by wine and milk.

> "Why do you spend your money
>   for that which is not bread,
> and your labor for that which
>   does not satisfy?" (Isaiah 55:2)

While the people of the earth, wearied in the search for some escape from their mistakes, their sin and shame, cry out for deliverance, and resort to idolatry and superstition, God's invitation stands, unchanged and unchanging.

> "Hearken diligently to me, and eat
>   what is good.
>   and delight yourselves in
>   fatness.
> Incline your ear, and come to
>   me;
>   hear, that your soul may live;
> and I will make with you an
>   everlasting covenant,
> my steadfast, sure love for
>   David." (Isaiah 55:2-3)

This is the Eternal's great invitation and promise, and the requirement is that people really want to change their lives and sincerely seek God, who then will have mercy and "abundantly pardon." (Isaiah 55:7) Many people want God to do something *for* them, but this is possible only as they truly want him to lay hold of their lives and do something *in* and *through* them.

Second Isaiah's Prophecy

Returning now to the historical situation in which the Second Isaiah lived and to which he spoke, let us see his message in its projection into the future. The eternal God is like no other; he is the Creator and Supreme Ruler over all the earth. Those returning from exile were the remnant through whom the hope of Israel would be fulfilled. They, the true Israel, would be God's servant people, bearing the divine message to all nations. They would be the bearers both of God's judgment and the glad tidings (the "good news") of his mercy. He also portrayed the awesome idea that their very *suffering* (personified as the suffering of a person — "a man of sorrows and acquainted with grief" — Isaiah 53:3) would attest to their authenticity as bearers of the message. As the prophets had been threatened and persecuted so also had been their nation, preparing it for its divine mission to the world.

The people of Israel never accepted the divine role which the Second Isaiah saw for them, but in due course, some five centuries later, there came One, Jesus of Nazareth, who in his own person, mission and ministry did fulfill this amazing vision of service and redemption. Both Jesus himself, and his disciples who interpreted his life and work, made much of what the Second Isaiah had said. (See Mark 1:2-8; Matthew 3:1-12; Luke 3:2-16; John 1:6,15,19-28) So today in Isaiah 52:13-53:12 Christians see the vision of the Suffering Servant fulfilled in only One, even Christ Jesus our Lord.

Judgment and Mercy

What then is the message? Divine judgment and mercy are continuing realities. God made an enduring promise, "an everlasting covenant," with Israel but the true "Israel" is the faithful people of God in every generation. In this, through the New Covenant, there is to be found the nature and mission of the Church when it is committed and faithful to the One who was to come, and who did come in Jesus of Nazareth, God-in-Christ working through the repentant, the forgiven and witnessing community.

Is our congregation a part of this community? How much do we want, how fervently do we pray, and how well do we work for it to be a part of the body of Christ? Our hope and our salvation come from our Lord as we share in the community of the repented and the repenting, the forgiven and the forgiving, and the committed and witnessing community.

We gain the best understanding of God's mercy for us and others as we follow Christ in showing love (agape) and forgiveness toward others, even our worst enemies. Jesus taught this profound truth when he said, "Blessed are the merciful, for they shall obtain mercy." (Matthew 5:7) Again in the great outline of prayer, he taught us to pray, "Forgive us, as we also have forgiven." (Matthew 6:12) God's mercy is unlimited toward us but we must respond by the way we conduct our own lives including letting God's mercy toward others become also our mercy. To do otherwise is to suffer judgment for our hardness of heart. (Mark 3:5) Here in one great truth and experience is God's judgment and mercy!

The Cypress and the Myrtle

In our own lives and in the life of the world today, there is great — even critical — need for the cypress and the myrtle! Now, in all our relationships, is the time to plant and cultivate these in the place of thorns and briers. Let us do this among those with whom we share most intimately — our husbands or wives, our parents and children. Let us do this also in our neighborhood, our work, business or profession and in our responsibilities as citizens of a great nation. And, by no means least in importance, let us do this in our church. How easy it seems to be for thorns to grow up even among Christians! But how wrong, for we are called to be part of the very body of Christ on earth. For Christ's sake, therefore, let the church be the Church in the neighborhood, in the city, state, nation and world.

Now is the time to pull up and destroy the poisonous things that have been allowed to grow; and to give a good future a chance. In this we have the promise of the Eternal that faith and hope, goodness and mercy in the hearts and lives of people will be renewed. "And it shall be to the Lord for a memorial, for an everlasting sign which shall not be cut off." (Isaiah 55:13)

FOR THE DISCUSSION GROUP

Outline

I. The thorn and the myrtle.
   A. "Instead of the thorn shall come up the cypress."
   B. The thorns we plant.
   C. The cypress and the myrtle.

II. The second Isaiah.
   A. The three "Isaiahs."
   B. Second Isaiah — fifteen chapters full of hope and comfort!
   C. The Lord's memorial or "everlasting sign."
   D. God's invitation to all stands unchanged and unchanging.

III. His message in depth.
   A. There is the remnant through whom the hope of Israel would be fulfilled and bring the message of divine judgment and mercy to all nations.
   B. As the prophets had been persecuted so had their nation thus preparing it, through suffering, for its divine mission to the world.
   C. Jesus Christ fulfilled the prophecy and established the New Covenant.
   D. The repented and repenting, the forgiven and the forgiving, and the committed and witnessing community has emerged.

IV. "Now is the time to pull up and destroy the thorns; and give a good future a chance."

For Discussion

I. A sermon is born.
   A. Discuss how ideas come to us at unexpected times and places.
   B. Are thorns and myrtle symbols of judgment and mercy?

II. Biblical research opens new depths of understanding.
   A. Discuss as fully as practicable the historic setting from which the Second Isaiah comes. (See *The Interpreter's Bible*, Vol. 6, and other commentaries.)
   B. In discouraging times, how does it help to look back to the Old Testament prophets?

      C. How may we differentiate between the "dated" and the "enduring" messages in the Bible?

III. The role of the remnant.
      A. How else could the divine message be carried forward from a faithful remnant?
      B. Discuss how the Old Testament message is extended through Christ into the New Testament, the church in history, and today.
      C. How should we understand the role of the remnant in the existential church?
      D. How much are we a part of the repented and repenting, the forgiven and the forgiving, and the committed and witnessing community?
      E. Is the Second Isaiah's faith in the continuing rebirth of faith and hope, goodness and mercy borne out in history? If it were not so, how much darker would the world be today? And if it is so, what comfort and strength does it give us?

IV. What can we do for the removal of the thorns and the planting of the myrtle in all human relationships?

America's Thanksgiving Day
Read: Hebrews 11

All national holidays have their significance and are important but only two remind us of our unique heritage, our "roots" as a people. One is Independence Day or the Fourth of July; the other, Thanksgiving Day, goes back to the very beginning.

The 364 Year Story

The prologue to the story began before the Pilgrims first stepped on what has since become known as the shore of Cape Cod Bay, Massachusetts, on November 21, 1620. While still on the Mayflower, the small ship which had brought them across the ocean, the crew and the passengers held a meeting. Those who chose to remain in the new world made a covenant now known as the *Mayflower Compact*, the first provision for self-determining government in America. It was a simple, yet profound statement. It united all who signed it in courage and integrity. The following quotations from it are worth hearing again:

"In ye name of God, Amen. We whose names are underwritten . . . Doe by these presents solemnly and mutualy in ye Presence of God, and one of another, covenant and combine ourselves togeather into a Civill body Politick; for our better ordering and preservation and Furtherance of ye ends aforesaid; and by Vertue hereof to enacte, constitute, and frame such just and equall Lawes, ordinances, Acts, Constitutions and Offices, from time to time, as shall be thought most meete and convenient for ye Generall Good of ye Colonie, unto which we promise all due submission and obedience."

The first winter on that bleak New England shore was a dreadful time of hard work and of fear and illness during which forty-four of the 102 who had sailed from England died of a strange disease. Among the dead was John Carver, their first governor. Conditions improved, however, during the summer of 1621. Friendly Indians taught the settlers to hunt and fish, and the corn harvest was good.

In gratitude for still being alive and hopefully expectant for the future Governor William Bradford decreed that December 13, 1621 be set aside as a time, not for fasting, but feasting and prayers of thanksgiving. This celebration reveals much about these intrepid people. The women spent many days preparing food, baking and roasting. Children turned roasts on spits over open fires. Some eighty friendly Indians came to the feast, bringing with them wild turkeys and venison. Tables were set outdoors and, like one big family, the colonists and the Indians participated in a time of gladness. This went on for three days. That was the First Thanksgiving Day in America.

Although it seems unlikely that there ever has been a year when the Pilgrims were entirely forgotten or prayers of thanksgiving were not offered, a national observance of such a day developed only slowly. The custom of observing a Thanksgiving Day (on varying dates) spread throughout the New England colonies. During the Revolutionary War eight special days of thanksgiving were observed. President George Washington issued the first general proclamation for such a day on November 26, 1789. Although, from time to time, some state governors issued such proclamations, the next presidential action did not come until 1864 when President Abraham Lincoln called for such an observance on the fourth (later changed to the last) Thursday of November. For the next seventy-five years America's Thanksgiving Day was celebrated on the last Thursday of November. Then in 1939 President Franklin D. Roosevelt set the observance on the third Thursday of November, in order to help business by lengthening the shopping period between Thanksgiving and Christmas. Controversy followed and some states chose to keep the traditional date. In 1941 Congress ruled that the fourth Thursday of November would be Thanksgiving Day.

Sojourners in a land of Promise

This national holiday not only takes us back to the beginning of our American ethos but interprets that heritage as nothing else can. The Pilgrims were Separatists in England, Christians who rejected the practices of the established Church of England, and, for that reason, were persecuted. In 1607 and 1608 a small group of them who lived near Scrooby fled to Holland. Soon other Separatists joined them and formed congregations in Amsterdam and Leiden. In August, 1620, some from Leiden went to Southhampton, England, and after a short stay there set sail in the Mayflower on their great adventure.

Later, in the Plymouth Colony, Governor William Bradford, spoke of himself and the others as "pilgrims and strangers upon the earth," a reference to Hebrews 11:13. From this we have a clear indication of how these very early Americans saw themselves and the hand of God in everything they did. They were familiar with the Biblical examples of faithful men and women, and counted themselves among them. Like Abraham of old, by faith they had gone out, not knowing where they were to go and "sojourned in the land of promise" and "looked forward to the city which has foundations, whose builder and maker is God." (Hebrews 11:8-10) To be sojourners in the land of promise is to engage with others in high adventure and significant accomplishment. Life itself is essentially just this, but unfortunately many fail to see it or to throw themselves into it. The venture of great faith is a vital part of our American heritage which we need to cherish in this our own time.

Our Strange New World

We must now venture in a strange new world. With feelings of nostalgia we often look back and add glamour and glory to the past but, in doing so, we tend to cloud our comprehension of the present and future. We must realize that there were not only big changes taking place during each of the last four centuries but also that a momentous transition occurred between the first and second halves of this century. Only as we become aware of this *and are willing to face today's realities*, will we be able to cope with them.

Here we can only list some of the things which are shaping this strange new era:

1. OPEC made a far-reaching impact on the United States and other highly industrialized nations. The thirteen members of the

Organization of Petroleum Exporting Countries made the price of their crude oil sixteen times higher in 1980 than it had been in 1973. Because of the industrialized nations' dependency upon oil, this price rise precipitated devasting inflation, unemployment and recession.

2. Many business leaders have shown more interest in conglomeration, restricted marketing practices and immediate bottom-line profits than in improving their products and keeping the cost of living in line with what people can pay without incurring serious indebtedness.

3. The inevitable economic recycling problem between all nations, and especially between those highly industrialized and those which are not, has become much more serious. Poverty and hunger in the Third World have grown far worse during the last decade. The enormous debts owed by the poor nations to the financial institutions and governments of the richer nations undermines the security and threatens the future of both.

4. While serious tensions have enlarged between *East* and *West*, that is between Russia and the United States (the Warsaw Pact nations and NATO), tensions have also grown between *North* and *South*, that is between the United States, Canada, Western Europe and Japan on the one hand, and most of the countries in Asia, Africa and Latin America on the other.

5. Over all this world complex of difficulty and human suffering there is the staggering economic drain of vast armaments which also increases the catastrophic danger of an atomic holocaust.

Reasons for Thanksgiving

In view of all this and the prospect of difficult times for at least the rest of this century, what reasons can we find for thanksgiving? Let us list some of them:

1. Let the first one be the good foundation of our republic which we recall every Thanksgiving Day and Fourth of July, and which we *renew* every time we truly give thanks for them. We think of the Mayflower Compact, the Declaration of Independence, the Constitution of the United States, including the Bill of Rights and the Amendments enacted across the years, Lincoln's Gettysburg Address and his Second Inaugural Address, and the presidential and legislative actions and judicial decisions across the years which support human values, justice and equity.

2. Our nation has been preserved through the terrible trials and dangers of the Revolutionary War, the Civil War, the First

World War and the Second World War.

3. Constitutional and stable government has continued through many difficult and perilous periods, and forty presidential administrations.

4. In America there has been a record of strong identification with democratic ideals and human rights. Although at times seriously compromised, these principles are none the less woven into the fabric of our tradition. They still play an important part in our foreign policy; and within our nation, they make most Americans quite uncomfortable when they are violated.

5. We have been blessed with a large number of honest and concerned citizens in every region of our nation. In times of cynicism, which come to all of us, we may cry out, "Who will show us any good?" (Psalm 4:6 KJV) but actually we who care are not alone; we are numbered among many of like mind, heart and life.

6. And most important of all, we are able to be thankful for our awareness of, and strength in, God. For us and many others, the words "In God We Trust" are of central importance in our own lives and in our citizenship.

All of these are, indeed, reasons for thanksgiving and enable us to live into the future with hope and strength.

Our Need for a Day of Thanksgiving

To list reasons for thanksgiving is one thing, but actually to be thankful is something else. It is not easy to be honestly and humbly grateful but it is an attitude which we all need to develop, irrespective of our circumstances. It is an important human potential which may be learned. As we look about us and see someone who is "better off" we may feel bitter about our condition. On the other hand, if we look around and see someone who is "worse off" we may feel gratified about our status, and be thankful. Although common, this is only a very low level of thanksgiving, and will quickly be lost.

A national day of thanksgiving, when rightly observed, can be helpful to us all. It projects us into something much greater than ourselves. Thanksgiving Day, since it is truly a national holiday, is an ideal occasion for broad ecumenical gatherings. If we worship with Catholics, Protestants, Jews and possibly those of other religious persuasions, we become part of a much more inclusive fellowship. *We feel our relationship with other Americans before God.*

In these distressing times of unemployment, underemployment, and grave uncertainties, giving thanks with others, regardless of our own present circumstances, is an important way of coping with difficulties which might otherwise be too much for us. Let us think again of those Pilgrims. Almost half of their little band died that first winter. We can hardly appreciate what this must have meant to those who continued to struggle to survive. Yet they were able to give thanks the next December with prayer and feasting. They also had the grace and courage to invite their neighbors, the Indians, whom at first they had so greatly feared, to join with them and contribute food for the celebration.

Such faith and courage is needed again every day through the coming years. Let each one of us say, I am an American. I can and will rejoice with those who rejoice and weep with those who weep. I am a Christian and I can and will thank God for his mercies and blessings. I can and will "look up and love and lift."*

---

*From the hymn, *I Would Be True* by Arnold Walter.

FOR THE DISCUSSION GROUP

Outline

I. The 364-year-story.
   A. The Mayflower compact.
   B. After the first winter, the first Thanksgiving in America.
   C. How the national observance grew.
   D. A part of our American heritage which should continue.

II. We venture now in a strange new world! Major problems confront us in these last two decades of the twentieth century.
   Consider:
   A. OPEC price rise precipitated devastating inflation, unemployment and recession.
   B. Conglomeration, restricted marketing practices, high union demands, and immediate bottom-line profits have resulted in inferior products and inflation.
   C. Economic recycling problems between nations, and poverty and hunger in the Third World, have grown much more serious.
   D. While high tension continues between east and west, other serious tensions have grown between north and south.
   E. The staggering economic drain of vast armaments continue and increase the danger of an atomic holocaust.

III. Reasons for Thanksgiving. Confronted by such difficulties and dangers, what reasons may we find for thanksgiving?
   Consider:
   A. The good foundation of our republic which we review every time we give thanks for it.
   B. Our nation has been preserved across the years through terrible trials and dangers.
   C. Constitutional and stable government continue.
   D. In America there has been a long record of identification with democratic ideals and human rights.
   E. We are blessed with a large number of honest and concerned citizens.
   F. The words, "In God We Trust" are of central importance in our lives and citizenship.

IV. The need for a national day of Thanksgiving.

A. America and each one of us need to be honestly and humbly grateful.
   B. We need to feel our relationship with other Americans before God.

For Discussion

I. A national Thanksgiving day nourishes our "roots."
   A. Discuss the Separatists in England. What other colonists came with strong Christian faith? And with democratic ideas and aspirations?
   B. Study the correlation between the development of this observance of national thanksgiving and historic crisis situations or special occasions. A review of presidential proclamations is interesting and revealing of times, circumstances and values.
   C. Is the annual observance becoming more or less meaningful and helpful in these changing times? How many look upon it as anything more than a "fun" holiday? The First Thanksgiving was a *feast*, but how did it differ in other ways from today's observance?

II. Understanding our own times is difficult.
   A. Is the prospect really for "difficult times" for at least the rest of this century?
   B. Review carefully the five areas of difficulty described (and possibly others not listed) and ask the above question about each.

III. We are still sojourners in a land of promise.
   A. Evaluate each of the reasons for thanksgiving.
   B. What other reasons may be added?

IV. Rediscovering old ways and discovering new ways of observing Thanksgiving day.
   A. Traditionally it was a time for family get-togethers. Today it is much more difficult to get to "grandma's house" but cards may be exchanged, telephone conversations may be shared, pictures and tape recordings may be sent, etc. Discuss these and other possibilities.
   B. More inclusive religious observations are planned in many communities, but they reach only a fraction of the population. How may the number and meaningfulness of such celebrations be increased?

C. In stressful times how may we learn more about our neighbors' condition and share faith, hope and love?
D. What more can we do to make us "proud to be Americans"?

The Kingdom, the Power and the Glory

Read: Matthew 6:1-15 and Luke 11:2-4

When we say, "I believe in God" what do we mean? Some people, if they are honest with their doubts, may answer: What I mean is that I am inclined to think that it is possible that there is an overall *something* which may not inappropriately be called "God." We must be honest with our questions and doubts but I hope that all of us have moved to a point in our thinking and living far beyond this. How does one affirm his or her faith? Certainly not only in words but also in acts and most of all in daring trust. The committed Christian bets his life — all that he has and all that he is — on God. Every day, and through all the years, *we who believe* do this, and must do this. Therefore we are fortunate if our daily venture in faith and trust is surrounded by a well-authenticated and time-tested relationship with our Heavenly Father.

Jesus gave the Lord's Prayer to his first disciples, and through them to the world, in answer to their plea, "Lord, teach us to pray." (Luke 11:1) It is best understood as an outline of prayer which is remarkably inclusive when it is studied carefully.

1. Jesus taught his disciples to pray in the *hallowed* name of God, our Father, who is none other than the absolute Supreme Being back of the whole cosmos and in, through and beyond all human life.

2. He taught us to pray for the Kingdom of God, that is, the doing of God's will, or *the fulfilling of the divine intention*, everywhere on earth.

3. He taught us to pray for our daily bread (and all other needs) *remembering* everyone in this earth's teeming and hungry multitude in that prayer.

4. He taught us to pray for the forgiveness of our sin and for *our willingness to forgive* others.

5. He taught us to pray for deliverance from evil by not seeking, *nor countenancing*, temptations to linger in our hearts which can only weaken or destroy our commitment not to sin.

Then, as we all know, the Lord's Prayer concludes with a doxology expressing three great affirmations: *"For thine is the Kingdom, and the Power, and the Glory, forever."* What is not so widely known is that this declaration is quite possibly not part of the original prayer given by Jesus. It does not appear in the Gospel of Luke, nor in some of the earliest manuscripts of the Gospel according to Matthew. If Jesus did not use the ascription, we can but wonder why he did not give it a more liturgical ending, and how these words became affixed to it. Here are two considerations:

First in order that prayer may come from deep in the mind, heart and will of the one who prays and not be a mere useless repetition of words, he said, "When you pray, go into your room and shut the door and pray to your Father who is in secret; and your Father who sees in secret will reward you." (Matthew 6:6) In this way he emphasized how sincere and personal must be our use of the prayer-outline he gave. We must not merely recite the Lord's Prayer, we must *pray* it.

Second, might it not have been the genius of our Lord to leave the prayer *incomplete* so that his disciples could have the joy and the courage to finish it with their own great affirmations? No Christian finds the fullness of strength and happiness in prayer until he makes his response to God, with praise and thanksgiving, for his life in Christ. So it may very well have been that the first disciples *learned* to make their response. In this they recalled prayer passages in the Hebrew Bible. Had not David prayed, "Thine, O Lord, is the greatness, and the power, and the glory, and the victory, and the majesty; for all that is in the heavens and in the earth is thine; thine is the kingdom, O Lord, and thou art exalted as head above all"? (1 Chronicles 29:11) Also, the psalmist had written, "They shall speak of the glory of thy kingdom, and tell of thy power . . . Thy Kingdom is an everlasting kingdom, and thy dominion endures throughout all generations." (Psalm 145:11-13) What is certain is that the now familiar ascription was part of the Lord's Prayer in Christian worship by the second century.

For Thine Is the Kingdom

What is the essence of the Kingdom of God? The answer is: God *over* all! God in all! And God *through* all! "In him we live and move and have our being." (Acts 17:28), that is, our very existence physically and spiritually. Often we seem to think and act as though we had to choose between interest in and support of the Kingdom of God or interest in and life in this world. What is wrong with that? Everything! These two must be brought together because they belong together. Sacredness and secularity coalesce in the Kingdom of God, and are there transformed.

Our Christian faith is well-established in human experience. We know both good and evil, love, and hate, and the redemption of people as well as their destruction. The building blocks of life are on the side of goodness, love and redemption. Like the buttresses of a great cathedral our faith and hope are supported by the historic life, teaching, ministry, death and resurrection of Jesus Christ. Therefore, as we live our lives we may verify the reality of the Kingdom of God in our own experience.

Humankind had not yet known the terror of the atomic bomb when T.S. Eliot wrote,

> "This is the way the world ends
> Not with a bang but a whimper."

But which is worse, death through meaningless existence and boredom or by catastrophic fire? We must not choose either one.

By its very nature, the Kingdom of the eternal God cannot be limited to earth time and space. Let us put this in perspective. Let us suppose that intelligent creatures inhabit other planets in this vast universe (which is most likely) and one of them developed a "civilization" on that sphere as humankind has done on the earth and then ceased to be. Would we then have to conclude that development had no purpose or lasting significance? Surely it would be most presumptuous and absurd to come to any such conclusion. Rather, with the vision of a Kingdom encompassing the whole cosmos, it could be affirmed that the life on that planet had been significant and that those who had responded to the will of the Eternal still continue through the provision made for them. Such are the outer reaches of our Christian affirmation of the Kingdom of God. Nuclear war may make the earth uninhabitable, but not even the BOMB can destroy the Kingdom of God in its cosmic dimensions.

For Thine Is the Power

The power of nature is enormous and awesome. We think of volcanoes, earthquakes, tornadoes, tidal waves, and the like. We tend to associate such naked fearsome power with God. And he who made the cosmos must be acquainted with such vast physical power and very much more. This, however, is not the kind of divine power which is most significant for us.

Let us recall the Old Testament account of how the discouraged Elijah fled into the wilderness and there observed "a great and strong wind which rent the mountains, and broke in pieces the rocks . . . but the Lord was not in the wind; and after the wind an earthquake, but the Lord was not in the earthquake; and after the earthquake a fire, but the Lord was not in the fire; and after the fire a still small voice," saying, *"What are you doing here, Elijah?"* (See 1 Kings 19:11-13) Many besides Elijah have heard the voice of God in their souls and have recognized this not only as the presence but also as the power of God to change them and their world.

The power for which we need to pray is not to escape from difficulties but rather to enable us to live honestly and courageously in the real world. In these days, all of us have become far more aware of the energy crisis. It is a fact, it is serious, and it is going to be with us for a long time. Still more serious, however, is the crisis in spiritual power. New forms of energy and other solutions to our many problems depend upon clear thinking, moral integrity and concern for others. This is where we need the highest and most important kind of power, the light and strength within our very being.

Which is the real person in us? Socrates said that each one of us is like a charioteer with the task of driving two horses, one gentle and tame, the other wild and undisciplined. The wild one he likened to our *passions* and the other to our *reason*. William Barclay, for many years the well-known Bible commentator in the Church of Scotland, reminded us that this very issue is dealt with throughout the Bible. Which is the true David? The David who spared Saul's life with amazing magnanimity and who would not drink the water which his mighty men at considerable risk brought from the well which was by the gate? Or the David who callously arranged the death of Uriah that he might lustfully possess Bathsheba? (See 2 Samuel, Chapters 11-12) Which is the true Peter? The Peter who denied Christ in the courtyard of the High Priest's House or the Peter who, for Christ, took his own life in his hands before the Council, declaring, "We must obey God rather than men." (Acts 5:29) Which is the true John? The John who wanted to call down fire from heaven to blast a Samaritan village or the John who had but one great message: "Love one another." (1 John 3:11)

So we examine ourselves. Which is the true man or woman in each of us? Barclay said, "There is only one person who can control the evil side of us, and who can make the good supreme, and that is Jesus Christ." This is the power we need, the power for which we pray, and the power we affirm. It is for this that Paul, in his letters to Timothy, his younger fellow minister, called upon him "to rekindle the gift that is within you . . . for God did not give us a spirit of timidity but a spirit of power and love and self-control." (2 Timothy 1:7,8) Let the great Apostle say this to each one of us!

For Thine Is the Glory

There is a sad and melancholy strain running all through human experience. This is to be seen in the often repeated theme of ancient and modern music and drama as well as in the day-after-day experiences of children, youth, active adults and senior citizens. It seems that we human beings cannot, for long, know joy without also knowing sadness. This is true because both joy and sadness have a common root in our psyche, in the inner feelings of our being.

If we care deeply, and we do, we will know happiness and unhappiness, success and failure, hope and disappointment. As we said, the power for which we pray is not for escape from difficulties, for this is impossible, but for the grace to live honestly and courageously. Fortunately, however, this is not all there is to it. As we live our lives as Christians we come to know an abiding strength and peace. If God has been welcomed in our lives, and if he has been with us through many, many experiences, we begin to sense something of the surprising glory of life.

What is God's glory? Where do we see it? In the heavens, yes! So said the psalmist of old. So also say men of science today. Many of us have watched the "Cosmos" series on TV, in which modern astronomy pictures the universe, and we have seen how more awesome the truth is than any science-fiction. Neverthless, as absolutely tremendous as this is, there is much more to God's glory. The Second Isaiah saw God's glory in the midst of daily human experiences. He wrote, "The Lord hath . . . glorified himself in Israel." (Isaiah 44:23 KJV) In parallel fashion, we may say that God glorifies himself in America, in our community, in our church, in our family and in our own lives.

Eternal life is not something that begins after death. Rather, it is something which may begin now and will transcend death. The human being, as a physical organism, is, of course, mortal. But the human being, as a spiritually disciplined soul, is immortal. We are citizens of the Kingdom which is not of this world alone, nor are we circumscribed by and limited to this world. Jesus said, "Whoever lives and believes in me [that is, who enters into the Kingdom of God] shall never die." (John 11:26)

I believe this. I hope that you also believe this, and that it will give you strength and joy all through the years — and forever.

So it is that the ascription to the Lord's Prayer becomes *our affirmation of faith*: "Thine is the Kingdom, the Power and the Glory, forever." It is the great swelling chorus across the ages, and into all the future of our Christian hope and trust in the living and eternal God.

FOR THE DISCUSSION GROUP

Outline

I. I believe . . .
   A. The committed Christian bets his life — all that he has and all that he is — on God. *We who believe, do this.*
   B. The Lord's Prayer is remarkably inclusive. The outline.
   C. Why didn't Jesus give it a more liturgical ending? Two suggestions.

II. For thine is the kingdom.
   A. Its essence: God *over* all! God *in* all! And God *through* all!
   B. Sacredness and secularity coalesce in the Kingdom of God, and are there transformed.
   C. Our faith and hope are supported by the historic life of Jesus Christ.
   D. The Kingdom of the Eternal God cannot be limited to earth-time and -space.

III. For thine is the power.
   A. The power of nature is enormous and awesome, but this is not the kind of power which is most significant for us. Elijah learned of the "still, small voice."
   B. More serious than the energy crisis is the crisis in spiritual power.
   C. Which is the truer man, the truer woman? "There is only one who can control the evil side of us, and who can make the good supreme, and that is Jesus Christ."
   D. This is the power we need, the power for which we pray, and the power we affirm.

IV. For thine is the glory.
   A. Both joy and sadness have a common root in our psyche.
   B. As we live as Christians we come to know an abiding strength and peace.
   C. God glorifies himself in the heavens, and in our own lives.
   D. Eternal life is not something that begins after death, rather it is something which may begin now and will transcend death.

V. The ascription to the Lord's Prayer becomes our affirmation of faith.
   A. It is the great swelling chorus across the ages, and into all the future of our Christian hope and trust in the living and eternal God.

For Discussion

I. Our daily venture in faith.
   A. How well-authenticated and time-tested is our relationship with our Heavenly Father? How may our experience and trust be improved?
   B. There is so much in the Lord's Prayer, as an outline of spiritual guidance and experience, that it is helpful to separate it into its categories. For example, have times when alone or with others to pray only, "*Our Father who art in heaven*" and elaborate upon what it means to be in communion with the Creator of the universe; and express praise and thankfulness! Then, at some other time, move on to the next category, etc.
   C. Explore the explanations suggested as to why the prayer ends so abruptly. Are there other possible reasons?

II. The kingdom of God.
   A. In "Our Father's World" can anything be altogether secular?
   B. Discuss again the great importance of the *historic* life of Jesus Christ.
   C. Discuss how not limiting the Kingdom of God to earth-time and -space increases our vision, faith and hope.

III. The presence and the power.
   A. Is God (the Holy Spirit) manifest in our consciousness and conscience? Does he speak through our awareness of right and wrong, our love and forgiveness, etc.? Discuss Elijah's experience; also the importance of letting the historic Christ speak to us through the Scriptures.
   B. In human situations, does "spiritual power" have to control "physical power," or will serious problems develop?

IV. The glory — divine and human.
   A. As we live as Christians, are we coming to know an abiding strength and peace?
   B. What does it mean that God glorifies himself in our lives?

C. Discuss the idea of "eternal life" beginning now.
V. Our personal affirmation of faith.
   A. Discuss how we may affirm and re-affirm our faith through many experiences.
   B. Do we feel that we have been led?
   C. What joy and strength is there in joining the "great swelling chorus" across the centuries and today?